The Song Atlas

JOHN GALLAS was born in 1950 in Wellington, New Zealand. He came to England in 1971 and currently works for the Leicestershire Student Support Service. His previous Carcanet books include *Practical Anarchy* (1989), *Flying Carpets Over Filbert Street* (1993), *Grrrrr* (1997) and *Resistance is Futile* (1999).

Also by John Gallas from Carcanet

Practical Anarchy
Grrrr
Resistance is Futile

The Song Atlas

A Book of World Poetry

edited by John Gallas

CARCANET

First published in 2002 by
Carcanet Press Limited
4th Floor, Conavon Court
12–16 Blackfriars Street
Manchester M3 5BQ

A CIP catalogue record for this book
is available from the British Library
ISBN 1 85754 614 8

The publisher acknowledges financial assistance
from the Arts Council of England

Set in Monotype Dante by XL Publishing Services, Tiverton
Printed and bound in England by SRP Ltd, Exeter

Contents

Khwaja Abdullah Ansari (1006–1089)

I came out of the unmade ...

I came out of the unmade,
and put up my tent in Bodily Woods.
I travelled through Mineralia and Vegetableland,
whence my brain brought me to the Animal States.
I continued, beyond there.
I minded the pearlshut drop of myself
in the sheerglass shell of a human heart,
and moved into the Prayer Hotel.
Then I continued, beyond there.
I took the way to Him.
I was a workman at His door.
Then our difference was unmade,
and I wondered into Him.

Anonymous

Exiles

Himare – black town –
Himare – 120 bells hang
in your churches –
why don't they ring?

Himare – are you struck dumb –
Himare – with fear
of the Vizier?

Strike – ring – dumb
bells – ring – Himare –
strike!

Hm. Now, brothers,
I have this hankering,
this wistful itch,
this rage
to wander around
Barbaka –
to drink
from the
Fita.

Kateb Yacine (1929–1989)

hello

hello my life
and you my despair –
here I am again at the nothings
jeering my heavy blues.

and you, my old madhead –
I brought you back a slice of heart.

hello hello you lot –
hello my old shadows –
I come back to you
like a lonely hell-seen trooper
and I know what screwy songs
will spook-swirl up tonight –
there's the mud-cranny
where my high proud forehead slept
in hurly winds
through December's tears –
that's me, my life,
collected in dust.

hello, all my things –
I've followed the tropic-bird
on heaven's wanders
and here I am blooded
with damage
fix-grinned in my heart.

hello my lead horizons
my old madlonging dreams –
hope flowers that way
in my rotted garden –
laughable torment
I open my beak
to fall flapping in thorns.

hello my pointless poems.

Josep Dalleres (*b.* 1949)

Museum

heavy
footsteps of
the coming day.
wornout
edgelines on
the road.
tattery
flap-shoes
with walking
so long.
it was necessary
to change the layout
make avenues
streets
find new shortcuts
build a museum
somewhere to exhibit
two flap-shoes
tired of walking.

Antonio Jacinto (*b.* 1924)

Monangamba Estate

Here it never rains:
my sweat splatters the shoots.

Here ripe coffee
is the rubric
of my curdled blood:

coffee, fired,
milled, smashed dust,
black as the hired hacks.

Black as the hired hacks.

Ask the whistling birds,
ask the ramping creeks
and the wild landsent wind:

Who gets up first? Who drags to work?
Who humps there
bedrolls and branbags?
Who cuts, and harvests dirt?
Who earns corn-mould, fish-rot,
rags, chickenfeed
and coshes?

Ask.
Who raises the rice?
Who fruits the orange-wood?

Ask.
Who pays the Boss?
Who buys his sluts, machines
and Niggerheaded cars?

Who blossoms the whiteman?
Who fruits his guts, who farms his cash?
Ask.

And the whistling birds
and the ramping creeks
and the wild landsent wind
say:

– Monangambeeeeyeeeeyeeee ...

Just let me shin up a palmtree.
Just let me drink palmbrew, just drink,
and, out of my head, forget

– Monangambeeeeyeeeeyeeee ...

Anonymous

Plantain

Plantain suckers dib the dirt
and tip the crumbled sod.
Their questing noses, moistly new,
run at independence
with pushy pokes.

Each last, older inch
runs back and back and back along
the plantain's gnarly rootline,
purpose-pliant, tougher, cargoed,
greyhaired, benign, first-stock.

Alfonsina Storni (1892–1938)

What Would They Say?

What would the blank, pared People say
if – ah, one day, by some superhappy whim –
I dyed my hair mulberry-platinum,
wore a Greek jubbah, swapped my buncomb
for a halo of jasmine-forgetmenot flowers;
if I sang in the streets to the whirring of fiddles,
if I yelled my poems on a tour of the Squares,
my punch unpulled by mannerly brakes?

Would they come, streetful and streetful, and gawp at me?
Would they burn me, like they burned my weird sisters?
Would they bang the bells and stampede Mass?

I imagine it sometimes: and laugh quietly.

Silva Kaputikyan (*b.* 1919)

In the Sevan Mountains

Alone, and spun in spills of sunshine,
I stood astride the hush of Sevan's hills:
high, so high that an eagle
tipped my shoulder with his wing
while I stood whorled in scud-mist.
And the world looked mighty, mighty and endless.

Then, in a moment, unseeing the slow, still space,
I looked down – at a small house,
and tracks along a rutted slope –

And I needed people.

Anonymous

Thunder floats ...

Thunder floats
thunder revs
across sunblacked
riversand.

Thunder smacks
thunder burbles
out of boiled
squall-clouds.

A light-bolt
zaps the bushland.

The first squall-drops
pat the first squall-drops
pitter and drill
in boom-falls.

Georg Trakl (1887–1914)

Grodek

All evening the autumn thickets
clat-clat with things that kill.
A black sun grinds over
gold lowlands and blue broads.
Night runs on dying soldiers
and hushes the wild howls
of their burst mouths.

And a scarlet cloud distils quietly
in the willowditch, where a rancorous God
lives, and is dropped blood, lunar chill.
All roads go to black rottenness.

Under golden branches of night and stars
my sister's shadow
gutters round the speechless trees
and collects the souls of heroes,
the burst heads. In the bulrushes
the brown flutes of autumn coo.

Oh sublimer lament!
You altar of generations –
the hot flame of souls
battens on a wilder agony:
grandchildren unborn.

Khurshid-Banu (1830–1897)

To my Son, Abbas

I am crushed, burning,
day and night,
without you:
a careless moth
in a candle's stupor-fire.
You were made, cankered,
to die, like a rose:
and I knell like a nightingale
for its rose.
And my heart, that flew
in love's high-sky,
crashed, crack-winged,
into the earth.
I am crushed, crying,
by your remembered look:
ah, my sheer cypress,
cracked too soon, too soon.

Anonymous

Chickcharnies

The pinetree thicket dances
like a deck of sailors

its wagging tops knot-connected
2 by 2 may I please do.

Nested in each knot the babies
swivel their tiny red-aimed searchlights.

The branches do exercises.
I stroll along under strollingly.

Flickery families hang by their tails
and glitter like hangers on a coatstand,

looking flexing sharp bits
blinking flapping bleeping

and blithering. I stroll on along
under the jingling pin-lit pines

protected by my ruby handkerchief
and a bunch of xanthic flowers.

Salman al-Tajir (1875–1925)

Poet to a Poet

Sugar-bank of sweet thoughts!
You draw its coinage well.
Men's hearts glitter
in its brilliant profit.
Neap-sea of shuttled knowledge!
You man its dark deeps well.
Men's minds sail
in its tide of words.
Moon-light of quiet beauty!
You sow its godgleam well.
Men's faces shine
in its disclosing.
Burst-spring of always-making!
You play its busy water well.
Men's souls loose scent
like sweetbasil, bubble-shook, on its edge.

Shamsur Rahman (*b.* 1929)

The Strike

Today no anxious arms crowd the counters.
    No trod-on toes, no fidget-queues, no push-and-shove.
    No sexy-silver coins dance behind the grilles,
    no covies of notes dive at drawers like keen and frantic gulls.
    Today, heaps of flesh have disappeared, *puff,*
    from city streets and wynds. The city sleeps like a baby
    on its mother's breast, outstilling Rodin's *Thinker.*

Stillness: that collects in the poet's brain when he waits for the
    eleventh line's dim design when ten are wovenly done:
    that Mohammed carried one day in the ruck of his sleeve
    when he strode down a rock-thorned track to his cave,
    when he was hooded with spiders'-webs, when he had
    come from his hidingplace, when he had hidden from
    wild-dark flashing claws, when he lit God's word-star
    in his heart – the stillness that came today.

Mainstreet is a noon-torpid whorehouse.

Stillness: spikes the heart like a bayonet. One, two men –
    like paperbits wafted in the sighing street.

Today the petrol-pumps are empty and still. Right here in the road
    the sound of my own breathing startles me. Somewhere near
    flowers unfold: I hear the petals softly swish. And after so long
    the great bird-babble seems to have escaped from behind
    the black wall of trains. Before today I never knew so many birds
    noised such careless glitter in this city.

My visitor's eyes flit round: boyshadows flick in darker shadows
    in the still and quiet park. The blazing engines in mills
    and factories stand stockstill. A crane stretches her thin
    pipe-neck out of the National Bank window, eating the silence.

I walked down Dhaka's empty streets, imagining much
in the silent space. A goldfish jumped onto my fingertips,
swelled, and flickered off to a creamy garden to find
some new shape in its endless flower-gallery. While I walked
I rubbed out the signs and hoardings and put there,
shimmering, my favourite poems. At each streetcorner
I hung Picasso, Matisse, Kandinsky.

Four crossed streets like a broad forehead: the trunk-road,
the hazed wynd's waist, the ventriloquist-market – stillness
massed, caught beauty, like an angel in a stone heaven.

A cat pounced, lovesick, at the heavy sunlight on the rubbish-dump.

Today the people slept, noon-early, under trees, and forgot work,
forgot money: in pushcart shade, in separate warehouses,
on trolleys, still bus-caves, mattresses of silence. And the
whole hurry of verbs lay drowned in deep water, in a
mossed greenroom, like tortoises, jade-green.

Today, suddenly, my city has changed: completely, awfully.

Anonymous

doodle durdle

doodle durdle caw caw
doodle durdle doo

doodle durdle coo coo
doodle durdle doo

doodle durdle caw caw
doodle durdle blam

doodle durdle coo coo
doodle durdle bang

if a crow flies with pigeons
he gets shot too.

BELARUS

Janka Kupala (1882–1946)

Yelling-alive

Wolf wails or wild-wind screeches,
nightingale pewls or goose honks,
I don't care: it's my country –
fields, forests, rivers – Belarus.

Hillfull, stone-sown,
crops knee-high to a sparrow,
I don't care: lovepity its huts and barns,
ah, there's nothing like them.

My hut, my barn are thatch-touselled:
measly, to tell the truth –
but I log-on-logged them myself,
and stamped the cloddy floor.

My hut, my barn are thatch-touselled:
and bring, knocking, to my soul,
feelings, thoughts. I dream them, let them in,
heartguests like Belief.

The hut watched while I found God's world;
scampering out to my first schoolbooks,
minding grandad's yarns by twiglight,
strutting to the Big House to Work for Money.

My barn, where I swooshed the yearly hay and barley,
whispered I Love You to Zosia …
and, years later, raked grain-threshings with my children,
and, this year, sweated up the bath-house.

Near sadness, luckless often:
Zosia digs, the children are gone to the world –
but I'm used to it, somehow, this:
screwed in the earth like a root.

Ah, it tells you things – everything:
gnarled birch, century-oak,
winter-freeze, summer grass,
sheepfold, moss-rugged well,

creek burbles, garden greening –
holds my heart, friend, and soul.
I plant-and-planted it myself: twenty years
and it's a bosky park.

I'm used to it, somehow, this:
I know the numbers, apples, plums,
nights with Zosia, years before,
and all the dreams.

God, it's heaven, heaven
when springsun blinks – my soul gulps –
when birds churr, everywhere
amongst my garden.

Cuckoos coo my life-news,
blackbirds heck, nightingales pewl,
sparrows pipe and nettle-peck:
and sunshine warms, and warms.

Watch friend, field, pasture,
salt-and-pepper hay, tight ruts
where reapscythes whistled, ploughs grumbled,
where I worked all light hours.

A long, long furrow greened with oats;
here, nearer, furrows balled with potatoes;
there, further, rye-furrows;
there, there, fallow land, plain as a drum.

In the oats, bulbhead flax greens,
bright and high;
there, barley-beards, and there, further,
by the barley, a grape-plot.

Where I look – now you know –
is my country, my all-land:
the people? – hm ... later, later ...
they *haul* life.

You'd like it – field, forest, my greened garden,
goose honks ... well, who wouldn't.
And the wild wind screeches: I don't care –
it's Belarus, yelling-alive.

Emile Verhaeren (1855–1916)

Spade

Streams stop as ice: wind blanches the cloudbank.
East in the knotted clods of the field
a spade stands shivered,
grave and raw.

Trace a cross over the sallow earth
with your long-boned fingers
when you go past on the road.

The house is sogged green,
its two limes snapped.
Ash in the grate,
a plaster block still stuck on the wall
and Mary keeled on the floor.

Trace a cross of rest and light
over the houses with your long-boned fingers.

Toads cold dead in numberless ploughlines;
fish dead in the cold sedge.
And the hoot of some bird, sparer, thinner,
sparer, thinner – down there. Lifeleaving.

Trace a cross with your kind fingers
over the road.

A spider slubs a dust-star
across the stable's bare skylight:
the farm by the river crosses balks
through and through its sour thatch
like arms with lopped hands.

Trace a last cross with your hand
over tomorrow.

Two rows of trees and bald trunks
axed along wayless roads:
and the villages – no bells to bash out
the hopeless, hiccupped Anger of God
at an empty echo and its cracked mouths.

Trace a cross over four horizons.

This is the end of fields, the end of evenings;
in the black hole of sky sadness grinds
its black suns like millstones,
and only maggots teem –
in the guts of dead women.

East in the knotted clods of the field,
over the torn body of ploughlands
stands, and always,
the plate of sheer steel, the spine of cold wood,
the spade.

Anonymous

When a fish ...

When a fish
screws
slimy up
out of
the long
dark
river-
downness
and
bubbling
says
down
there
blub
in the
long
dark
deepness
blub
there's
an
alli-
gator
blub
oh
believe
that
fish.

Anonymous

Elephant

Big-ball elephant
sits like a hill:
Glory Enormous!
slapping his fear-fans.
Snaps trees, stamps fields,
rips up men like rags,
hangs them on branches.
Scram if you see him!
Glory Enormous!

Boom! Boom!
Scram if you hear him:
spiky-palm-cruncher,
ashblack earthquake.
Judders forests,
Glory Enormous,
stopless trampler!

Huntable at home,
by the fire;
shootable with stories –
but ha
a different story –
Glory Enormous!
Hello! Good afternoon!

Carries his head-load,
creaking his tree-neck:
Scram if you see him!
Death, don't chase me,
Death, don't swat
your trunk my way!

Glory Enormous!
Water-well eyes,
grave-girth teeth,
billhook tusks –
one squashes a carryman!

Man beholds you head-on –
sometimes:
man beholds you arsewards –
usually.
World-stamper, all-trampler,
Glory Enormous!
Leperskin-joint-rolled,
Boom! Boom!
Death, don't chase me,
Glory Enormous!

Anonymous

Dad is busy ...

Dad is busy.
His son is busy.
The fields are
rippled wet.

Dad is thinking.
His son is thinking.
The fields are
crackled dry.

Dad is busy.
His son is thinking.
The tiger muscles
through the wood.

Dad is thinking.
His son is busy.
The birds bank
in the blue sky.

They haggle, joke,
with other men:
when they talk to each other,
they will know more.

Ricardo Jaimes Freyre (1868–1933)

Night-time

Battered, black branches, gale-rattled; and
split-skewered trunks rearing, blustered and heaved; and
down amongst the moss, where night-burbles skim,
oak-roots crack out and jut, tearing the earth.

Cloudbulks rumble through the sky: hippogriffs,
chimeras, fangled sphinxes, fever-gods,
panicked unicorns and dragons who chase
the clotted roils of septic hydras; and
their limbs, ripped in the soundless struggle,
hood the sickly moon-front with a curdled blind.

Shadows zig from the old, stripped trunksplits and
flicker at the forest in a spooked race
over the moss, where night-burbles skim and
oak-roots jut and threaten.

Freak-things coiled in weird shifts
crack out of their frozen, factless graves
in the grim dream of an endless night,
while dragons and hydras boil in the sky and
their limbs, ripped in the soundless fight,
hood the sickly moon-front with a curdled blind.

Muza Cazim Catic (1878–1928)

Nostalgia

Way … way back … nine hills away,
there's a sleepy land, shining-charmed.
Way … way back … blue seas away,
lulls the land of radiant life.

Flowers glow there, lightlike
and the nightingale burns, lovesick, forever;
the flowers suck my lifedew –
ah, let me hold it tight!

It's evening now. In my room I can hear
a hidden voice calling me lightwards.
Way, way over the blue seas
moon-waves glimmer … longing …

my blue soul tips over them,
and floats …
floats nine hills away
to a lapis tower, shining-charmed.

Anonymous

Bushwoman stands here ...

Bushwoman stands here
Night hangs over her
Stars stab it

Hunter-stars
that rip night
take his heart

Bushwoman sings here
Night hangs over her
The land lies still

Hunter-stars
that stab night
give him yours

Bushwoman holds up her child
Night hangs over her
Ripped with stars

Hunter-stars
sky-hunters
give him your star-heart

Cassiano Ricardo (1895–1975)

Orchid

The orchid seems like
a flesh flower, like a mouth,
disquieting us.
Arachne's flower.

Humanish,
a mouth, but made
of milk-kind petals,
image of untruth.

Image of a word
wordlessly made.
Image of bad faith.

What will the humanish mouth
of the orchid
say?

Anonymous

A twist of hair ...

A twist of hair
stitches softly
puffed flour
on a pan.

I lower my
pinced fingers
at it in a thin
flour-cloud.

Carefully. The hair
must not prick
deeper or
slip away.

And the flour
must not hush
off the edge
by breath or dab.

A delicate matter
needs the same
exact line
to put right.

Atanas Dalchev (1904–1978)

Snow

Over strip-raked iron rooves,
over the metalled map of streets,
snow flicks, dab-settled white,
blotless, luminous, like
Godsworld ... here ... Hah. Never.
A leaden smog-drape enthroned
on the city tops ... yearlong, yearslong:
where winter is black and heavenwhite unknown:
where the blank sky drops dank drops,
minute-lives unmade
by police and whore-beats
in a smogbruised mush.
And chimneys soot the morning ...

White, still snow in the park ...
children lightly play ...

Anonymous

Cattle-count

1, the rust-red one, hide-gleaming:
2, the blackandwhite one,
   like a pied crow:
3, the zebra-hide, long belly-knotted:
4, the drab-spot hide,
like dibbled beans:
and 5, the best – my firecollared, wheaty-hide bull;
braw bull of my sonsy cows!

Anonymous

The Match that Darkened the Sun

The bush bangs
its branches flooded
with a roll
of smoke.

The straw house
crackles words its
breath a roll
of smoke.

I watch it fire
the air that
warps the roll
of smoke.

I hear my match
fired further shouting
in a roll
of smoke.

Yin Luoth (*b.* 1951)

Phnom Penh Morning

The green life brightens,
drawing its new, freshed air:
the sky, licked with lightest light,
lies long, milk-cool, unburned.
Birds stitch songs
into the city's first hum.

Breadmen hoot,
sound-sport with the birds,
their dittoed songs skirling
at the sky; and the city
winds into its day.

I think: this stitch, this bird-buzz ...
is it the need-pressed breadsong of the sky –
begging for the small, sold crumbs of life?

I think: this city – this cool-lit sky ...
how can they know each other's mind? ...
what words, what songs? ...
But try and know: by that we are more men.

Jean-Paul Nyunai (*b.* 1932)

An Hour of Life

What I want
Raab
what I want
isn't a fortune
or someone else's goodluck
Raab
what I want
is to be able to run my life
like a flat creek slips between its brinks
noiseless
you think these are chicken words
that a live body is nothing like
dead wood
I don't say it isn't
but can't you believe me back
when I promise you I've really thought like that
some days when confusion
stacks on my shoulders
like a thousand trucks jammed
with all the world's weight.

Alfred Des Rochers (1901–1978)

'City-Hotel'

Bags on backs, wrapped in red mackinaws,
brawny shanks clinched in bootlegs,
the going shantymen blow-out
before they go – to winter in Malvina.

In the bar, a sloped sunbeam blinks
through orange-madder panes
and golds the nickel-stools: where
a gin-sad johnny leans, crying.

Oldtimers gum and roar and caw
blubbery burdens from old songs;
but one newboy, funked in the row,

thinks he's in VanDyke's godforsaken camp
and swigs a halfschooner, watching
hoofers grinning from lacquered bills.

Corsino Fortes (*b.* 1933)

Island

Sun and spore: root and lightning:
sound-drum
blooming
round God's bare head.

Anonymous

2 Termite Skyscrapers

2
termite
skyscrapers

he tries
to separate
his
eyes

the man
who
minds
2
termite
skyscrapers

comes home
with
nothing
and
a
headache.

Anonymous

The Parts of a Thornbush

Under thudding cattle
the thornbush root does –

sieve, clutch, drink, take –
its absolute and lightless work.

Thornbush prickles sew the sky.
Cattle crackle, graze and grunt

the darted, light-sucking needles.
The thornbush root does –

sieve, clutch, drink, take –
its absolute and lightless work.

Carlos Pezo à Veliz (1879–1908)

Country Funeral

Down the graveyard track,
with a body on their backs,
the poor bearers,
thought-lost, advance:

four lanterns coming down
Marga-Marga towards the village;
four sad lights,
tear-flickering;
four oak-logs;
four old men ...

One tired voice prays
for the deadman's endless peace;
shifting sounds; grave,
weird tree-shapes;
wayoff, in shadows,
dog-yowls;
and the frail drone
of haunted echoes.

The wind heaves down. A voice says,
'Rain's coming.'
Another voice whispers,
'Pray for him ... pray for him.'

The dog-yowls skitter away
in wrinkled hillsides;
huge, unearthly, a hush
rolls down over the night.
The poor bearers
hurry their prayers
and one repeats:
'The rain's coming,
it's four o'clock, it'll soon be morning,
pray for him ... pray for him.'

And as the rain pricks down
I say goodbye to the funeral,
click spurs to my horse
and hurry into the mountains.

And there, in the murky mountains,
I wonder, who was he? and cry.
Some poor, unsung soul
who arrived one day from wayoff,
who loved the fields,
and the sun, and the track
that life quiets along, to its end,
where he, poor worker,
sick, tired and old,
found, one sunset, nothingness.

Chuang Tze (*b.* 370 BC)

Man

Consider: if we measured the Four Oceans
and compared the resulting area proportionately
with the combined extent of Heaven and Earth,
we could say that they are as the prick
of a mud-bubble in the Immense Marshes.

Consider again: if we measured the Present Kingdom
and compared the resulting area proportionately
with the combined extent of all Dry Land,
we could say that it is as a solitary
corngrain in the Enormous Granary.

Man is merely one of a prodigious number of
palpable objects: thus, if we consider man
proportionately with the absolute sum of such objects,
we could say that he is as a hairtip
on the rippling body of a mighty horse.

José Asuncion Silva (1865–1896)

Art

A poem is a holy glass – put
undiluted *thought* in it, only that –
in whose blinking drop images gleam
like the gold bubbles in an old, shone wine.

Tip in flowers – flowers that the endless, punching
chill of the world has bruised –
quiet memories of things that will never come back
and dewlicked roses.

Thus our brutish existence is made sweet –
as if with an unfathomable essence –
burning in the flames of our affected souls:
one drop of such matchless balm is enough.

Salim Hatubou (*b.* 1972)

Night 1

a light
in darkness
hold your breath
mouth the dove-song
look tie-down mad
sssh
your light
in darkness

Night 9

I took
the kings' yawl
I scudded out
to sea
but the waves
juddered
my hopes
so
I'm left
unsure

Jean-Baptiste Tati-Loutard (*b.* 1938)

Man-Myth: Puberty

Then,
there was a horizon of blue women:
the boy-sun,
speed-tired, slept in their arms.
Ah, it was perfect.
Then,
one wounded day,
his shade-stepping star
rammed a stone, and spurted all its milk.

Lisimaco Chavarria (1878–1913)

Lone Tree

The tree stands on a pike-top
against the wind's shock;
and hushes the howls in its woodthreads –
and sings when the wind whips it.

When lightning rips, madder and madder,
dazzling the bluewhite sky with snapping words,
it leaves the pother coolly alone
and wraps its hurt in unearthly anger.

The tree stands on a pike-top
against the lightning's snap;
and I look up to it in my long thoughts ...

I long for its flooding wood-light,
its glowing answer to unkindness,
spite and bitterness – silence.

Tin Ujevic (1891–1955)

green branch with a sadness of yellow fruit

In some old Split park
I daydream softly, my soul asleep:
green branch with a sadness of yellow fruit.
The damp dream sticks to my soul;
and longing shivers like a small, coatless bird,
like a snapped blue song,
like a wan, hopeless clogdance,
like a shoeless tramp on a stranded road.
My heart is seven scraps,
all fiery-skewered:
marble sways over my breath.
Blurry thoughts flinch in the lightquiver;
my blooded brain starts in its box:
above my dark your clement eyes
dazzle, and you are not here.

José Marti (1853–1895)

I grow a white rose …

I grow a white rose –
January, June, whenever –
for plainheart friends
who squarely shake my hand.

And for scurrile men
who root up my life's heart,
I grow – not a sting or prickleplant –
I grow a white rose.

Leonidas Malenis (*b.* 1937)

Hopeless Eveningsong

What's left, what's left of love
under the eucalyptus tree?
Just some sandy dirt.
The last fawnboy's gone:
kicking like a dead-age
jackal-bronze,
touching
Cyclops, Centaur.
Don't leave me. Don't go.
You
held youngness
on a gold string
and kept
the knife-thought of death
shut up in your fist.

Stanislav Neumann (1875–1947)

Winter Night

Not this world, but a dream.
Spellbound lustre-light
on glazed waves of fields
under the sky's black blind.

Not this world; not like it.
The air of white roads
that fetch stardazzle into their dip
to give their quiet shine.

Not this world, but a slip
of never-endingness.
And I dream of white forevers
in my own stopped shadow.

Kama Kamanda (*b. 1952*)

The Poet's Poem

Words gush out of his wrung soul's roots,
and wrap life's to a stranger's pains.
The poet's remains
are freedom, and the Truth-Thing hunt.
Like a storm through garbaged land
his poems beat our right-reluctant hearts.
Hope buzzes on his tongue
and his inside sun shines kindness
in the hiding-house of dreams.

Steen Steensen Blicher (1782–1848)

My birthplace is the brown heather-land ...

My birthplace is the brown heather-land:
the sun of my childhood days smiles on the bleak moors;
my callow footsteps are pressed in the gold sand;
my youngman's gladness is borne on the black uplands.

To me, the flowerless levels are beautiful,
and brown moors – as beautiful as the garden of Eden:
one day my bones, too, will stay there,
crossed with my father's heather-heavy grave.

Abdourahman Waberi (*b.* 1965)

between clackstones and sun-rule ...

1

between clackstones
and sun-
rule
all water drunk
all cavils kill
since sun-up
time
stakes this land:
split maul
in Africa.

2

racked geology
seen by
drifting birds
a shed skin
under each step
cloudless
ashy
moreless.

3

puffskite fire-hill
Ardoukoba
since it
woke
us up,
was man
too blockish
for you?

4

so the Prophet
palmed
Habash-land
– maybe in memory
of Bilal –
that doesn't
explain the
thorn-life
of *my* shore.

5

the herd
thinner
than others
and the men than
others too.

6

a port
a town
garrison
a mere
trainline
a spur
loaded they say
behind.

7

spare
style for
a runt
republic.

Anonymous

In the Woods

Blat ... blat ... water
levers leaves ...
trees shift
with an easy fever ...
insects tick ...

Scritch ... scritch ... cabbagetrees
fret each other ...
the fig umbrellas itself ...
an owl hoos
down the green dark ...

Spitter ... spitter ... swallows
slip through
the steel
white sky's
pieces.

Fabio Fiallo (1866–1942)

A Silence of Eyes

Your sweet black eyes, heavy with shade,
are a voice, oh my love.
My night-thoughts fill my heart with tears.

Your sweet black eyes are a voice
in the word-packed silence
that is you – so light, my ear mistakes
their landfall in my deep dark …

like two birds safe-walled
in a spiked rock on some unseen beach
that bell silent prayers at the sky,
songless in their thicket nest.

Anonymous

The Mauberes

far in the forest deep
in their own
words the
Mauberes rustle
bluegreen
leaves like
a dust-tapped
drum
the only
tell-breath of their
quiet lives

we passed them
we missed them
we hardly heard them
we left them
alone ...

the knot-track man
led them out only
once to lay
a tree-long gun down
in Time at the edge
of the forest deep
in their own words
the Mauberes rustling
round him like
bluegreen leaves
like fog

we passed them
we missed them
we hardly heard them
we left them
alone ...

and they whispered
like leaves
like a dust-tapped
drum *we don't need*
this we don't need
this we give up
war we give up
war their quiet
lives rustling
their own
words

we passed them
we missed them
we hardly heard them
we left them
alone ...

far in the forest deep
in their own bluegreen
words the
Mauberes rustle you
can hear them
whisper *this is*
peace this is
peace if you
listen to the
tell-breath of their
quiet lives

we passed them
we missed them
we hardly heard them
we left them
alone ..

César Davila Andrade (1918–1967)

The Abandoned House

(I went in twlight, while the sun was lost.)

An empty statue wept on the stoop.
Deep dragoons of dust stirred
at the wannest haunts of rot.

A shaded hole passed into nothing.

Emptiness moved in: murk-fleets
and mighty bells, already mute.

I heard a footfall gone to another age;
I saw the stump of my soul in a cistern.

A white wind numb and folded
in a dry sheet of forgotten birds;

a clock deep in acid;
the weight of a bird passing through the wall.

A dead girl dreamed in a story
breathed from a high brume-window.

An alphabet glided backwards,
dead-days first,
through a dwindled wicket of cards.

(I found these words on a white wall:
'7th March Maria Eugenia died.')

And above, in the afternoon, bishops floated
with lamps full of sulphur and wheat.
Above, in the afternoon.

It was not me who had come back
but a stranger that I weep to … sometimes …

and died in …

Anonymous (*c*.1550–1070 BC)

Brightlines

Mekhmekh flowers:
cool my heart.
When I'm wrapped in you,
I stow you coolly,
as they move me.

Seeing you
shines my eyes –
cool colours.

I fit with you
as they move me:
and look coolly
at my heart –
I'm wrapped in it:
it's you.

Our hour moves:
I need always
when I'm wrapped in you.

You shine my heart –
cool colours:
it was wan.

Seamu flowers:
stretch me.
I'm your wide sister:
and your garden,
pricked with seedbuds
and herbscent.

Your fingers dig,
delve a ditch in it:
cool in the windgust.

Your fingers wrap mine
when we walk in it:
it's me.
My heart stretches
to hold us:
it's you.

I'm wide enough
to hold your words:
pricked seeds.

You fill me:
more than meat,
more than milk.

Zait flowers:
heat my heart.
When you burn
on my bed,
bottle-keen,
I pull the wound cymes
off your hair
and dip my hot fingers
in your feet.

Alfredo Espino (1900–1928)

Sweet Pale Girl

Sweet pale girl – who begs
in bars – the cold sunrise
lights her on a doorstep –
small hands hard with cold, and blank-hearted.

Sweet pale girl – no past or place –
whose smile is a bitter stamp
of bleakness, minted in
her wide, deep-dark eyes –

whose skin is hunger-hung –
clouds watch her, and the night sky knows –
raining stars in this suburb's stillness.

Sweet pale girl – who no one knows –
and the muddied river drags bright stars along
in the hot, tired night.

Anonymous (10th century)

Riddle

My snout chews the field like a prow.
I dig, churn the way the treebiter rudders me
and rut the way my hunched boss shoves.

He shoves me down bulldozes behind.
I snout the earth, he bursts seed.

I came from woods: rattled out thumping,
knotted to his cart. I'm scarred and scar.

When I churn, dig, the way looks green
and cracked black. A shineshaped claw
knocked through my spine bites under me;

the same knocked through my forehead,
shoved sideways so my teeth bite,
tearing the fieldsea like a black prow
when my hunched boss shoves right behind.

Anonymous

Clothes

wild white dress
stuffed yellow shirt
squeezed green wrapper
ripped orange shift
floaty blue singlet
fretted brown gown
spick grey britches
patched black suit
split cream smock
throttled cherry pants
shrunk navy dungarees
gorgeous red pyjamas
droopy pink T-shirt
flash khaki coat
death is a thing
we all have to wear.

Anonymous

My wide eyes watch ...

My
wide eyes watch
the hollow sky through
my gap-split
soot-smut
roof

I
am a line
on my bed
fishing for sleep
straw-prickled
chaff-stunk

I
hold my careful
tears and
worldache in
shut in my
swollen eyes

My
wide eyes watch
the cold dreaming
moon easy
on its star-straw
air-squabbed
couch

I
am only
pain my eyes
sleep but my
gap-split heart
is wide awake.

Ernst Enno (1875–1934)

You Never Ask

Heads each on each, the numb flowers drowse:
winter and night, winter and night still.
Under the snow lifesparks zip
and busy in awakedness.

Heads each to each, the raw flowers swell:
and grass and seedears, grass and seedears –
sunshine, big blueness,
and the world bowling along.

You never ask
why the world goes on, on like that:
sunshine, business, death, living,
a High House, then a dump.

You never ask
why the world goes on, on so blind –
and where God has turned,
turned his love-eye.

Anonymous

The Coffee Rancher

I'm a Coffee Rancher.
A Man of Substance.
Coffee.

Money steams
off my hands,
coffee-rich.

The sea dances
past my lawn,
coffee-frothed.

Gammymen clutter my door.
I give them money,
coffee-scented.

Orphans tickle my door.
I give them money,
coffee-balm.

My unrottable shroud
hangs in the hall,
coffee-strong.

When I die
I will go to Heaven,
coffee-radiant.

I'm a Coffee Rancher.
A Man of Substance.
Coffee.

Anonymous

Kadavu

Kadavu:
sandbay
the east wind
cools:
dropped mango
on rockplates.

Christmas is gone,
New Year is coming:
and I walk it
unworried.

Daylight dips
away, sun-shrinking:
songs shift in
the filling
dark.
*Some unworded
heartscalm fills
this place.*

The sea runs
its smooth reaches
at the bay:
menfish softly
dive in
its tissue.

Christmas is gone,
New Year is coming:
I can hear
falling fruit.

Daylight dips
away, light-leaving:
songs shift in
the long
dark.
*Some unworded
heartscalm fills
this place.*

Katri Vala (1901–1944)

Bridge

I wish my soul was an unmoved boulder –
yet I nervy-wait the day I am lifted of its load ...
shivering child-hands, here, there,
snatch my hand:
a million panic souls yell
and my heart shakes with them.
I love people: but I dread
they will be One Man,
they will be One Suffering.

I wish I was an armed sea
to wreck the wall
that shuts people
from the highsun land.
I am only a shook bridge
on Man's road.

Jules Laforgue (1860–1887)

Pierrot Says

I – merely a moon-mimer
making rings on silver pools …
so … with no more intent
than to become a legend.

I kilt my creamy mandarin sleeves
with mutinous poise:
I oo my mouth and – blow
tender instructions from a Crucifix.

I – become a legend, ah yes,
on the doorstep of quack centuries.
Where are the dear old years?
When will God be recast?

Léon-Gontram Damas (1912–1978)

The Wind

Wide sea – black night – I woke up lovesick –
hands full of nothings –
with all the wind's words –
and a ship heaves the seaspume and goes –
rolling – goes to its end –

wide sea – black night –

the wind remutters its homework –
the wind sighs at buried treasure –
the wind flutes its vespers –
the wind is a jail full of madmen –

wide sea – black night –

and a ship heaves the seaspume and goes –
rolling – goes to its end.

Anonymous

Sun

Dead darkness falls
headlong falling
at your flashlight glare
your beam-eye arrows
shot from your fire-box:
flare-shots
rip her coat
pitch-coat pricked
with star-studs:
your flare-shots
rip her pitch-dark coat.

Anonymous

Sleep-song

Sleep and sleep well, little one:
but open your eyes
and look at me for a minute
before you go to sleep.

I want to see the thing
the thing that shines inside
inside your clear new eyes
and shines at me.

Now shut your eyes, little one:
I think I saw
what I wanted to see.
Sleep now, and sleep well.

Anonymous

Suliko

I looked for my love's long-home.
Sadness tangled my heart.
My loveless soul like lead.
Suliko, where are you?

A nightingale sang like light
in the blue, muskrose shade,
and I asked him where oh where
he had hidden Suliko from me.

The nightingale stopped singing
and touched the rose with his beak:
Here, he said, *she's here:*
still in the deep blue shade.

Ludwig Holty (1748–1776)

Legacy

To my friends. When I'm dead,
hang up my meagre harp
on the wall at the back of the altar,
with the blinking deathwreaths
of a hundred cold girls …

The beadle grins at his tourists
and points at my meagre harp
and tickles its knotted pink streamers:
and they whisper
under the golden strings.

Sometimes, he confides with big eyes,
the strings sing by themselves,
piano, like bees, in the orange evening.
The children, charmed from the graveyard,
come in and watch the flowers shake.

Anonymous

This song explodes

This song explodes
with others' beat-bursts, others' names,
Hammer-Singer, bird-blood promises,
force-stepping, others' sway.
This song explodes
with hyena-yawls, wordwar-yawls,
watchdogs' yammer, thunder-yammer.
The SongGod swims down: other singers,
KO-Singer, Thunder-Singers, burst me –
Start war! Beat for war!
Bright for war! Sing!
Other singers, song-men,
I sing the dust that fawns your feet,
I sing no death, no sickman's song –
this bright song explodes!

Georgias Drosines (1859–1951)

Wild Creeper

The wild creeper noses up
in the air and next to it
a bramble scores its prickled stalks
along the dark clay.

The wild creeper pours
shoots on him, to hide
the bramble's thorns
with shiny milk-bloom.

He stops scratching in
the dark clay, uncranks,
and noses the wild creeper
as she spills on him.

I was a wane-pricked whin
before you loved me,
sweet wild creeper,
sweet milk-bloom.

Your white arms all
undid my bramble thorns
and gentled me
inside spilling shoots.

This unlikely company
we have kept:
your easy beauty
and my ugliness.

Anonymous

The candy-throated Carib flaps ...

The candy-throated Carib
flaps along the treetops

brushing heaven and
the ceiling of the world

its eyes eating
the crammed air

like years like certainty
like years of certainty

like colour like kings
like breath flaps

along the treetops brushing
heaven and the world

The candy-throated Carib
lies on the cut field

weighed in mud and
the stubble of the earth

the ants eating
his full eyes

like years like nothing
like years of nothing

like colour like kings
like breath lies

on the cut field weighed
in mud and earth.

Roberto Monzon (1948–1992)

Opaque Copper

The darkfall of your voice is tired:
and sounds like opaque copper, or chafes
like chest-stones;
and makes a dulled thump
that dies, echoless,
in tonight's flat air.

Keita Fodeba (1921–1969)

and it's morning ...

The small village that danced all night
wakes up, slowly here, slowly there. Herders lead
their flocks into the valley to the sound of reed
pipes; still-sleepy girls follow one another
along the winding track to the spring. In the
Holy Man's yard a group of children round a
woodfire murmur chapters from the Koran.

(*Gourd-harp music*)

and it's morning ...

Battle of day and night. Darkness dies, slowly,
tired of the fight. Already,
on the horizon, a few red-licked sunbeams
light up the last clouds like huge bunches of
flametrees in flower.

(*Gourd-harp music*)

and it's morning ...

And down below, in the middle of a wide,
crimson-circled plain, the outline of a bending
man clears the ground: the outline of Naman
the farmer. With each swish of his cut-stick
the frightened birds take off and fly away
with wild wing-beats to the quiet banks of
the Djoliba. His grey cottony pants flatten
the grass, soaked with dew. Deft and
tireless, he works to make sure his seeds
are planted by the first rains.

Anonymous

To me, your beauty ...

To me, your beauty, breathstop-young,
is like a lime swinging grassland
after rain, where prismed steam
unlooms its light.

Anonymous

Mango

In the fat, green greenery
that slaps lightly in the light,
a mango bobs,
like a floating boat
in a greeny wave.

Just a bit along the branch
a parrot parrots:
floffing feathers, clacking beak,
knowing wrinkly wink
and mostly mum.

Flapaflapaswoshabomp!
A macaw lands
in the fat, green greenery,
rather near beside the mango
that bobs lightly in the light.

His glassy eye eyes the parrot,
bobbing with the bobbing mango,
all whistling-innocent,
all burbling-occupied,
just a bit along the branch.

Oi, says the macaw, *Ark! Ark!*
The parrot necks his neck,
all calm-surprised,
all oh-who's-that,
and mostly mum.

The mango bobs the bobbing birds.
They eye it, glassy-eyed,
and shuffle, softly, attention-
otherwisedly, at it.
What, says the parrot.

That mango, says the macaw.
Oh what mango, says the parrot.
That mango by your foot.
What oh by my foot,
oh, haha, says the parrot,

That *mango. Yes,* says the macaw,
is it ripe? They bob bobbingly
in the bright green sea
and the mango bobs
like a floating boat.

Well? says the macaw.
Grbidugfuiethdkhsl, says the parrot.
I beg your pardon, says the macaw.
The parrot peers at his claws,
all burbling-occupied.

The mango bobs
golden-rusty in the green greenery,
like a floating
golden-rusty boat
in a greeny wave.

Grbidugfuiethdkhsl, says the parrot.
The macaw eyes the parrot
uneasily. *Could you please,*
says the macaw, *tell me*
if that mango is ripe.

The parrot necks his neck,
all calm-surprised.
Grbidugfuiethdkhsl, he says.
Grbidugfuiethdkhsl! Grbidugfuiethdkhsl!
The macaw sidles one sidle away.

The mango bobs. The macaw's
glassy eye eyes the parrot.
Oi, says the macaw. *Ark! Ark!*
The parrot peers at his claws,
all whistling-innocent.

Flapaflapaswoshazipfff!
The macaw takes off,
muttering mutteringly.
The mango bobs wildly,
with a wild, golden bob.

The parrot winks
a knowing wrinkly wink
and bobs by the mango
in the fat, green greenery,
and mostly mum.

Léon Laleau (1892–1979)

Hot Ports

The battered packets pull out for faraway thought-places,
and pull my heart out with them:
where the sky is always blue, dabbed with
balm-clouds, and life is never sad.

Women cram the jetties.
The steep ships hoot and crackle.
Torn handkerchieves wave goodbye,
and the wet-faced hopefuls go –

awake with happy fear, and the old dreams' doing,
awake to the wild names, thought-names ...
the sea is silk ... lapis ... dapple-shot ...

The battered packets thrum through dusk to the sea
and the faraway, spellbound, golden ports ...
Brindisi, Auckland, Havana, Melbourne ...

Clementina Suarez (1902–1991)

A Workwoman's Death

I'll go down to my grave unbroken.
My teeth are fast and bright;
my muscle tight; my whole stuff limber
and my head high up, up.

I'll go down to Death bloom-mouthed;
with a clear and unshaken-said Yes.
I know all my minutes are counted,
and Life never stalls its end.

I'll go down to Its darkness unshocked:
please, no tears for that.
My bubbled blood ebbs like oil,
and now – hush.

Don't tidy my hair;
don't cross my arms on me:
leave me the way I die,
and let me go down to my grave unbroken.

Don't show me for Death, overclothed, remade;
don't give me to die what I never had.
Sweet friends that are nothing new
can take me to my grave, and dig.

Don't eat to remember me, or cross my grave.
I want what the poor get – no more.
And my hand will be fisted from Death to Death
and my name in the wind like a flag.

Nagy Laszlo (1925–1978)

Who'll Bear Love

When I'm drowned in days and gone
who'll be here to cheer the cricket-crowths?
Who'll huff fire on frost-prickled sprigs?
Who'll nail himself up on a rainbow?
Who'll hug rock-hips and blunt them with tears
into a pasture of waves?
Who'll be here to nuzzle hairs and arteries
twining out of boulderwalls?
Who'll put up a cathedral of bluewords
in the name of restive faith?
When I'm drowned in days and gone
who'll be here to scare vultures away?
Who'll bear love in his teeth
across to the other, far side?

Snorri Sturluson (1179–1241)

Corpsebeach

I have heard of a crannog
on Corpsebeach.

Venom splats
its walls are pleached

Promise-splitters
must crawl through

cut off from the sun
Its doors gawp north.

out of its gable-slots:
adderbacks.

and life-snatchers
its clotted gutters.

Ghalib (1797–1869)

Ghazal 13: 'Where are your woo-trysts …'

Where are your woo-trysts and your heart-wrenches now, Ghalib?
The days and nights and months and years of it all? Gone. Finished.

Who's got the time to practise love?
The frenzies, the ogling and the heartthrobs? Finished. Gone.

Love, friends, sprouts from the ecstatic conceit of A for B;
ah, such young-sprung grace, such mind-gush is finished and gone.

It's tough to weep tears of blood;
the sturdy heart, the brave purpose are gone and finished.

Now your body is a chickenbag, Ghalib;
the world's Great Branching Means are finished and gone.

INDONESIA

Chairil Anwar (1922–1949)

Light Leaving a Small Harbour

for Sri Ajati

No glow of promises this time
amongst the warehouses, wood-houses, rig-masts'
sad stutter. A beached bumboat, sealess ship,
prows at the dark, tugging, burring.

Thin rain and lightleaving. An eagle pitches;
flaps in dark thoughts, and out, coolly, day –
out to other love. Still. Still.
Now, coast and sky shut down with the waves.

Nothing. Only me. Walking.
Looking for elsewhere, promises taken,
promises lost; giving them up, here,
on Beach No. Four, the last gag of poison.

Saadi (1194?–1291?)

Prayers

My shoes are mulberry with dew.
My hat catches the first pins of light.
The lining of my coat buzzes blue.

Morning empties down me:
a sloe drink drunk
out of a lemon glass.

I light up like a candle.
Through the rosebushes
heatless flames lick life at me.

I hear a nightingale
turn my orange tree gold
with gentle complexity.

My shoes are black with dew.
I look up: the lime treetop
pipes with language and light.

Uneasy, peeved, stung, galled,
hurt, crabbit, I slash the dew
with my shoes and stamp inside.

Morning yells white in my garden.
The nightingale bursts glass fluteballs
against the ravished palate of the sky.

Bah. Why, says my friendliest friend,
who is twirling his coffee in my arbour,
are you so uneasy, peeved, stung, etc.?

As I was born a man, I answer crabbitly,
I am ashamed of my silence
when a bird can sing such songs at God.

Partridges hoot from the hills.
Frogs gulp in my glittering pond.
I am ashamed of a moment's silence.

Abu Nuwas (756–813)

The Party's Over

The party's over. The bursting zanies and their night
have whitened away. The place is spent and still.
Dragged drinkpots' blunted wakes rut the sand
where fallen hats of flowergrass blur and blink.

I always ask What lasts? the morning after.
I stopped someone: Wild, I said, wasn't it?
And only a booming silence round Sabat
could tell me who we'd been.

One heady day. Two. Three. Four. Five.
Gone. And now we softly go ...

Drink wheeled in a gold quaich
arted round almost to life:
King Khosro on the front, for the sides
his men, butting at bayed animals.
Drink swam at its top studs,
water frothed, gasping, on its edge.

Anonymous (11th Century)

Copier

My hand's crabbed up with scribbling.
I can't steer the prickly pen
and it splats plum ink
like a skinny spitting beak.

A runny restless gill of Godness
twines out of my nutslim hand
and reels its plum holly-sap
around the aching paper.

And I haul my skinny splatting pen
along a whole holiday of bright books
to fill Sir Splendid's orders –
so my hand's crabbed up with scribbling.

Anonymous

Dancer

Come back, come back again,
Shulam girl. Come back, come back again
so we can watch you wind
the Mahanaim dance,
so we can watch –

your thewed feet leafed in shoes,
your willow thighs like milkbeads
made by a glass master,
your navel bulbed
as a tumbler bubbled with wine,
your spine like a rick of wheat
swaddled in lilies,
your breasts like twin gazelle-bairns:

your neck is an ivory keep,
your eyes are the Heshbon wells
that gutter by Bath-rabbim,
your nose is the gatewatch of Lebanon
looking down at Damascus,
your head dizzies like Mount Carmel,
your soughing hair is a mulberry wood
where a man is lost.

My pulse is a storm.

Your whole swayed height
is as sinewed as a palmtree
and your breasts are sound as fruit.

Let me swarm up the palmtree,
grabbing its limber flags;
your breasts will be
like clutches of grapes,
your breath like wrung apples
and your mouth like wine ...

... that will slip swelling
over his sleeping mouth.

Salvatore Quasimodo (1901–1968)

O my Dear Animals

Autumn smears the green hills,
O my dear animals. The last wheep
of the birds, the boom of the slatey heath
that slides at the spun sound of the sea
will break again. And the woodsmell
in the rain, and the marlsmell of burrows
kick against the houses here,
where men are, O my dear animals.

The face that winds its eyes hugely,
and the hand that draws where
a drill of thunder snaps the sky
are yours, O my wolves,
my foxes scorched with blood.
All the hands, and all the faces are yours.
It's all been useless – living,
the days and days worn with hard cold water
while children skirl in a garden.
Miles from us now.
But they smear in the sky
as soft as shadows.
It's your voice.
And I know that it's all unhappened.

Anonymous

The Death of Old Men

Old Henri is dying.
Children play tag in the dust.
And we, whose world is next,
sit with him under the tree
and watch his knowledge burn.

All he said: like a dictionary.
All he did: like an atlas.
All he was: like a library.

Old Henri is dying.
Youngsters fight in the grass.
And we, whose haul is next,
sit with him under the tree
and watch his knowledge burn.

All he thought: like an encyclopaedia.
All he imagined: like a storybook.
All he was: like a library.

Anonymous

work's end

Ah Miss Claire
come with me
the evening breeze
is smooth and cool
let me lift
your basket down
and come with me
Miss Claire.

Ah Miss Claire
come with me
breeze yourself
and please yourself
your donkey-day
thank God is done
and come with me
Miss Claire.

Ah Miss Flo
come with me
the evening breeze
is smooth and cool
let me dance
your day away
and come with me
Miss Flo.

Ah Miss Flo
come with me
the mountainside
strolls up the sky
your donkey-day
thank God is done
and come with me
Miss Flo.

Ah Miss Martha
come with me
the evening breeze
is smooth and cool
let me cook up
something sweet
and come with me
Miss Martha.

Ah Miss Martha
come with me
let me light
your freedom fire
your donkey-day
thank God is done
and come with me
Miss Martha.

Princess Nukata (*fl.c.*660–690)

A Polite Debate

Winter's hobbles break
and Spring drives out!

The cold-dumbed birds
break out their skirls;
and limetrapped blossoms
burst their swollen stalks.
I hurry out, but misfind
the flowers in their skein-lushed lawns,
the less-light blossoms
ravelled in the grass.

But when I see
leaves littering the autumn hills
my hands shake,
quick-scarlet with their leafload,
and I love a little less
the green ones on their branches.

To me, the green time is not so completely perfect:
If pressed, I would choose the autumn hills.

Anonymous

more than love

I sit on the lemon
verandah of heaven
and watch the lights below

I loved my necklace
but my neck more

The darkbright ghosts
of careful men
gloop like oil in water

I loved my bracelet
but my wrist more

Creeks of honey ooze
in gullies of basilled grass
touched by more than music

I loved my ring
but my finger more

love gave me them
Love gave me this
Love gave me more than love

I loved my heart
but my soul more

Abai Kunanbaev (1845–1904)

Summer

Summer climbs the mountains.
Flowers overcolour and blanch.
Men leave the sun and sit,
tree-tented, by the cold creek.
Horses bray, each apart
in the warm air, and the long grass
whiffles in a lime plain.
Hushed and still, the horseherd stand
in wither-high water; and wave
the flies away with silk-swish tails;
and colts clatter the air,
rippling the quiet, and lifted eyes.
Geese hoot through certain blue.
Ducks slip past, water-brushing.
Girls frame the tents, their
soft voices melting in the heat.
The boss rides back from his sheep,
smiling through tent-town,
clopping with warm slow time,
his hat a tilted effect.
And old-timers suck round
the milk-hooch bag, their
say-again stories fired
in their laugh-again eyes.
The stewmeat steams.
A boy tugs his mother's spoon.
The bosses sit in a curl of time
on light-swirled carpets
under a languid tilt
and suck their tea and talk and talk
in mannered turn. A rheumy old grouch
shouts at the shepherds' dust,
one ear on his own brave show.
No other ear hears more than heat
and quiet: and talk runs on,

creek-like, with the creek.
The herdsmen, strutting-young,
rock coolly in their saddles, parading back
from night-time grazing, dressed
to see, and riding twice their blood.
Way past the tents in the softened heat
the boss's son casts falcons
with his friends. Their horses mouth
the close, bright air. The bird
drills up along the sky
and nails a heat-blown goose.
And the rheumy old grouch,
coughing in the shepherds' dust,
stares, unwatched, and hot with sadness
that his glory is all gone.

Anonymous

Smalltown Yala

Yala, this song's for you, Yala,
your song – O O O

O all the little accountants are
scribbling scribbling
here
very busy
here
very very busy
here

O Adoray's dress is flowers
on the outside
here
and plain
here
on the inside
here

O Amara's mum can't afford
a bike
here
so she walks
here
and there
here

O the Kamnaras bowl round
on bikes
here
there
here
and everywhere
here

O Oloo Nyabondo drummer
has given up trains
here
he's so busy
here
so very busy
here

O will they let Oloo drummer
on a plane
there
it's so busy
there
so very busy
there

Yala, this one's for you, Yala,
your song – O O O

with all your little accountants
scribbling scribbling.

Anonymous

I funnel up ...

I funnel up,
earth-leaving:
I snap the palm flags
on the way.
I peer at the sky-forever.
I see two red clouds.
If they were nearer
that would be my song-colour.

Anonymous

I thought for ten years ...

I thought for ten years, then I made my house:
one room for me, one for the moon, one for the wind.
No room for the mountain, no room for the river: they are my
outside home.

Cho Myong-ni (1697–1756)

The sky-geese have gone ...

The sky-geese have gone, high away;
hoarfrost is here;
autumn's nights are long, long, long,
travellers' hearts blue and bluer.
My moon-honeyed garden holds on,
rueful, gentle: my home, my state.

Anonymous

come – go ...

come – go –
here not too
long – there
not too
long – bee-
like

the yellow
head – the red
spike – the
orange – catkin

come – go –
sweetly – here
not too
long – sweetly –
there not
too long

don't lick
your
honey-friends
away

Anonymous

Mother, and Given Girl

I hung foxfur	on the door
and shook	bloodless-faced
go	*to him*
My tentpole	sky-lifting
my hawk	spring-shining
go	*to him*
My milk's	cream
my tongue's	fizz
go	*to him*
Grown	in softness
grown	unfrowned
go	*to him*
Smile	at trouble
smile	at him
go	*to him*
My day	light
my summer	green
go	*to him*

Anonymous

Soul Call

Come quick
down dim tracks
stubble-tracks
come quick
out of unblazed bush
and salty flats
come quick

Come quick
past cobra-grass
shining grass
come quick
through tiger wood
jade wood
come quick

Come quick
through rivers' swell
cold swell
come quick
past calling songs
charm-songs
come quick

Come quick
to the sturdy woodwalls
and bowed roofridge
come quick
to the open eyes and mouth
of your home
come quick

Ojars Vacietis (1933–1983)

Goodbye to a Spaceman

It's me, child:
your planet, Earth –

I can't promise
my radio-waving
will get to you every time, and everywhere:
I can't promise
my rocket-steel
will last –

but you will:
because you're my child –
and when that faith fails
it fails in my own grey crowns and clouds.

I'm untorn when a train leaves,
unsick when ships slip out:

but when your rocket fires
my childlove
will blaze …

I'm your mother:
no one can ungrab you
from my arms.

My love
will not loose you in your rocket;
my gravity-grip
will drag you back
with sweet greed.

'Don't go!'
don't listen.
'Come back quick':
do that.

Come back quick –
with star-flakes on your boots.
Come back quick –
with stars blinking in your eyes.
Come back quick –
with star-nerve in your heart.

My sprung tracks plash
along my creekbanks,
and rainbrightness pours down –
and my lilacs
will unloose their sweet smell,
breezed with stormfresh ozone,
like your lovegirl's opened hair.

It's me, child:
your planet, Earth –
take from me
on your starry course
a ryeloaf
and a clod.

Ahmed al-Barbir (1747–1811)

Ah, Mr Businessman!

Ah, Mr Businessman! Nothing but a heart-bank.
Faith-in-profit: despair-in-loss.
Bank on Faith-in-God-
and-Prophet! A lossless business.

Anonymous

Peace, Rain, Plenty

Mountains plumb.
Bush whispering.
Men unnettled.
= Peace.

Dust gurgling.
Green bubbling.
Men dazzled.
= Rain.

Roads rolling.
Men coming.
Men going.
= Plenty.

Anonymous

bird and man

when a bird flies out
a bird notifies no one
a bird noises nothing
a bird newses no one
a bird announces nothing
a bird lugs no luggage
a bird humfs nothing
a bird carries no clobber
a bird totes nothing
a bird parades no pedigree
a bird trumpets nothing
a bird broadcasts no business
a bird rattles nothing

when a man sets out
a man notifies everyone
a man noises everything
a man newses everyone
a man announces everything
a man lugs luggage
a man humfs everything
a man carries clobber
a man totes everything
a man parades his pedigree
a man trumpets everything
a man broadcasts his business
a man rattles everything

Ibrahim al-Osta Omar (1908–1950)

Not Quiet

shut up they said
I said I am not a block
shut up is for blocks
words words action action
that is living
that is God's figure-of-fight
my heart beats
I am not a block
my tongue works
words words action action
that is living
shut up is for blocks
nightingales sing
high in the hills
down in the valleys
that is living
that is God's figure-of-fight
no matter what happens
I am not a block
not quiet not shut up
a birdcage
shuts up
no bird
not shut up
everything
living
life
death
everything
comes
not quiet
from
God

Michael Donhauser (*b.* 1956)

The Quince

First, I think, like a pear, velvet-furred; a liquid bite,
I expect; scent and sap.
All teeth and kisses to eat, I think; sucked and oozy;
scent of it, thirst for it.
Then it's hard, uneatable, wooden, fruitless, potato.
It's a bearable imposture: put it on a cupboard,
smell it again and again – sucked and oozy again,
I think.
It spreads its promise sweetly there, absorbing
reeks and rumours.
To make it eatable: cut into slices, boil – all day –
with plenty of sugar.
Then its mushy mass will serve up, as if in echoes,
its promise – the quince-fruit.

Justinas Marcinkevicius (*b.* 1930)

Prelude to 'Blood & Ash'

There's a village and there's no village.
And its people burnt with it.
The yet-to-live,
the yet-to-die,
the yet-
to-be-born.
There's a village and there's no village.

No!
There *is* a village –
there!
still burning, always burning,
will burn, always will
while the fire-butchers
stay alive.

Open up, fire!
let me in,
so I can see who's burning.
There's the boy – once
he said to me:
'I need my life, so I can live.'

He wanted alot – and so little.
Brother, sweet friend, why
why didn't you say:
'I need my life, so I can *fight*.'
Heat blasts in my chest:
what's burning? My heart.
Burn, always burn, always will
so people won't – ever – again.

There's the farmer – he was ploughing,
ploughing the winterfield, shoving, slogging –
they stopped him. The furrow halfditched.
He rammed the plough in the earth –
it's still there.
Unrusted.
Unrusted – because
each night the farmer comes back to his field,
rolls up his sackpants,
crosses himself, and ploughs.
And his furrow goes on and on,
Pirciupis, Panerai,
Auschwitz, Mauthausen.
On and on, long as life,
like life, on and on,
undoing death's darkdug trenches.

Be unrusted always.

Marcel Gerard (*b.* 1917)

Flow

Woman walking out of the water
undone by your plunge
cut by your lick-limbed stroke
where the fond sea wraps you

Woman walking out of the water
you unscrew your black hairknot
you twist it like a gloss
python the shine wraps you ...

French-made face
flicked with a know-it eye
glowed as wine

I remember you
bronze unspoken woman
sweet reopened dream.

Kocho Racin (1908–1945)

Tobacco Pickers

Bronze stones and cold scales:
but they'll never weigh
our tobacco-bane,
our salt sweat.

From night-blurred summer daybreaks
to godforsaken winter lightdeaths,
tobacco drinks our pain,
sweat, blood and strength.
Our faces thin, and a bronze weight
sits cold on our hearts.

First light, dew-wet, we're there,
bent double in our home-fields,
automatic pickers:
leaf, leaf, pick –
leaf, leaf, tie –
leaf, leaf, turn over, push down –
leaf, leaf, thread – patient, sad –
on long sweatbead strings.
Rage and hope and hate,
milk-blind eyes stare
at leaves, leaves, paper-bronze,
the hard pages of an unlucky life.
Tie, next, tie, next, quiet, necessary.
Now you know.

It's weigh-up day.
No scales will do it: this bane
pushes on and on into the heart.
Nothing can balance it:
not sadness – but rage;
and into our milkblind eyes
its storm wells up.

The scales hold bronze leaves
and in our hearts rage the great storms
of bronze sadness, bronze tobacco,
bronze salt sweat from our hands.

Jean-Joseph Rabéarivelo (1901–1937)

Cactuses

Throng of hand-casts
holding flowers at the cyan sky
throng of unfingered hands
fixed in the wind
some close-cupped wellspring
stirs in their shining palms
some close-held wellspring
that waters the crowding cattle
the crowding changing droves
of south-border men.

Unfingered hands, deep-sprung;
hand-casts, crowns of the sky.

When the City's sides were green,
green as leaf-lit moonbeams,
when the Iarive hills were bare,
hunched bare like bullbacks,
they hid on rocky steeps too steep for goats
holding their wellspring close,
flower-decked lepers.

Root out the spring of their deformity
in the caves they came from –
a spring dimmer than evening
and further than morning –
and you'll find what I know:
that earth-blood, rock-sweat
and wind-sperm,
stirring together in their palms,
have rotted their fingers
and put on gold flowers instead.

Anonymous

he is handsome ...

he is handsome
he is happy

she is rainsoft
she is rich

they are starbrained
they are strong

better to copy
than to envy
them

better to copy
than to envy
them

Anonymous

love's footprints

When you're gone
we'll salaam
the foot-flattened
grass.

Anonymous

The Muiveyo Cow

Long ago, when the Sultan sat
on his Sultanic Seat
and ruled
with a kind of
fatherly fright,
herds of cows
happily wandered
and munched
the island of Male.

The Sultan's Sultanic
Herd wandered and munched
with a kind of
special wandering, munching
Pride
of Place
and the people
treated them
with a kind of
winking respect.

Now, one day
the Second Secretary
of the Sultan's Sultanic
Secret Service
found a cow
from the Royal Herd
swimming
in a mooing kind of way
round and round a blue lagoon
at Muiveyo
on the other side
of the island.
Swimming and mooing,
in fact,

in a kind of
frightening way.

He hurried back to tell the Sultan,
who was sitting
on his Sultanic Seat
and ruling.
'Heavens!' said the Sultan.
'Call the Royal Sultanic
Council Cabinet Consultative
Commission!'
And they did.

And the Royal Sultanic
Council Cabinet Consultative
Commission
discussed,
in a lengthy way,
how to save the cow
who was swimming and mooing
in the blue lagoon
on the other side
of the island.

However,
although they
discussed the matter
in a lengthy way
for a long time
they came to no
agreement,
conclusion
or decision.

The Sultan said,
'Send the Second Secretary
of my Sultanic Secret Service
back
to the blue lagoon
at Muiveyo
on the other side
of the island
to find out

in a more informative way
about
the mooing and swimming
of my Royal Cow.'
And they did.

The Second Secretary
of the Sultanic Secret Service
was gone
for a long time.
When he returned,
the Sultan said,
'What did you find
at the blue lagoon
at Muiveyo
on the other side
of the island?'

And the Second Secretary
of the Sultanic Secret Service said:
'The cow
has finished his swim.'

The Royal Sultanic
Council Cabinet Consultative
Commission
sighed
in a smiling kind of way
and dispersed
to play draughts.

And the Sultan's Sultanic Herd
happily wandered
and munched
once more
the island of Male,
and the Sultan sat
on his Sultanic Seat
and went on
ruling.

Anonymous

God Knows Why

the unaccountable trip
the sudden sway

a big hot bird
rustles like paper

the hopeless fall
the unlooked-for shutdown

the hot mud breaks
for the dropped lamb

the bird winds out its neck
its eyes blank white like pebbles

the cool compliance
God knows why

the blind vulture
breaks from its branch

MALTA

Dun Karm (1871–1961)

Polestar

When I'm bored with work
I leave the city fire-factory,
go north, and stare at the polestar,
age-still and bright.

Glittered sisters linedance
past, beam-winged,
measured by their mother's thought,
their careful, star-cool hub.

Moveless zero: it steers
shipmen to their soulkept ends
clear up past storms
and thrashing dark.

And when coiled waves tip
some father, some brother
out on a cold, fell shore,
it sparks his hopeful blood.

Anonymous

The First Coconut Tree

Ebon, fruitfilled Ebon,
and Moniak most of all.

The woman's sand-womb failed.
The man speared her.

He flung her in the sea.
She like driftwood.

Ebon, fruitfilled Ebon,
and Moniak most of all.

The woman luffed slow
to a sandbank and stayed.

And lived there in the cool
of a bowing tree.

Ebon, fruitfilled Ebon,
and Moniak most of all.

And one day she bundled out
a boy and a coconut.

Which grew: one a bigger boy,
the other a coconut tree.

Ebon, fruitfilled Ebon,
and Moniak most of all.

And they made nut-husk weave,
and nut-shell buckets:

and the boy caught
a sea-cucumber in its root-net.

Ebon, fruitfilled Ebon,
and Moniak most of all.

The woman's brothers found her,
and told the boy *carry the cucumber*

round all the islands, run,
and stamp on it on each.

Ebon, fruitfilled Ebon,
and Moniak most of all.

And where he did a giant split
of coconut trees trunked up,

and breadfruit trees,
and in the blue sea, fish-flashes.

Ebon, fruitfilled Ebon,
and Moniak most of all.

And the woman's brothers went home
and left them magicking on Moniak,

where they lived in the cool
of a bowing tree.

Ebon, fruitfilled, Ebon,
and Moniak most of all.

Oumar Ba (1900–1998)

Seen to be Done

Bashed up?
Robbed?
Hospitalised?
Witnesses?
Swarming like sandgrains.
Kadeel is one,
Ndulla,
Ndiam Bele is one,
even the birds can bear witness ...
but ah, you forget: the chief
has his son for a judge
and his daughter's man
for translator.

Malcolm de Chazal (1902–1981)

it was / so hot ...

it was
so hot
that
the flowers
had
to use
their
colours
as fans.

Juana Inés de la Cruz (1648–1695)

World! why do you hound me?

World! why do you hound me like this?
Do I annoy you? Really? When all I want
is to put Beauty in my Understanding,
and not my Understanding in Beauty?

I have no interest in Money and Luxury:
it gives me more satisfaction
to put Wealth in my Understanding
than my Understanding in Wealth.

A Pretty Face is soon gone:
how can I value the daily loot of Time?
or the forged crown of Luxury?

For as long as I look for Truth, I believe
it is better to unmake the vanities of Life
than to unmake my Life with vanities.

Anonymous

Paddle-song

Birds, we're birds,
deep-flying
in the seasky,
high,
blue.

Birds, we're birds,
deep-flying
in the sprayclouds,
high,
white.

Spirits, we're spirits,
deep-flying
in the manless water,
high,
air.

Spirits, we're spirits,
deep-flying
in the bluewhite air,
high,
beyond.

Mihai Eminescu (1850–1889)

Goodbye

From now till never, goodbye:
goodbye, from my blindsdown eyes:
I leave the world
to you.

From now till never, do what you want:
goodbye, I leave you my worldknot dream:
my world is leaving
me.

Goodbye: from once till now –
and now no more –
dizzied with star-sparks
I waited,

glittered, cold, intent
by your window,
breathing through branch-twists, waiting
for you.

Ah, from once till now
we were happy: walking the world
in hushed moon-charm
together.

And I whispered night to lie
from once to always
so I would always be
with you:

and save each word
from the time-crumpling air:
words I hardly
remember.

And if these rippled traces
surprise me now, they seem
like a story from some
never-once.

And if the moon charms the grass-flats
and ripples the thin water,
it seems an age of lives from once
till now.

Goodbye, from my blindsdown eyes
who see a new no-moon:
goodbye: you are once, and I am
nothing now.

Louis Notari (1879–1961)

A wee bird sang in the wasteland …

A wee bird sang in the wasteland,
and I said to him: Little friend,
I'm happy to stay for your concert,

though I'm sure you're not singing for me …
and if Love inspires you, poor thing,
then leave off your little tweet-gush:

can't you see in this blasted place
no one will ever sing back?
In a twinkling, the wee bird

raced into song again, but
in whispers, as if he wanted
to unsecret something to me.

Can't you see if I wanted
to sing out of passion or pride,
I wouldn't be singing here?

You see, while I'm whistling my song
I'm not thinking of nests or fat feathers …
I'll tell you: I might be little, my friend,

but I'm trying to sing to the glory of God.

Dashborjyn Natsagdori (1906–1937)

My Country

Khentei, Khangai, Soyon – awe-rearing ranges:
northside wonders – timber crowds and treethick heights:
Menem, Sharga, Nomin's silence – the still Gobi Desert:
southside seas of sand, and on and on:
they are my home: Mongolia, full-souled and fine.

Kherlen, Onon, Tuul – purebright rivers,
creeks, runnels, springs – purebright drink:
Khovsgol, Uvs, Buir – broad, deep,
rivers, lakes where men and animals drink:
they are my home: Mongolia, full-souled and fine.

Orkhon, Selenge, Khukhui – brightest rivers:
ranges and heights where metals and stones stand under:
broken past-places, keeps and camps,
highroads, pathways to far, far places:
they are my home: Mongolia, full-souled and fine.

Awe-rearing heights, snow-shining:
unridden endlessness under blue sky:
purebright heights, endlessly far:
and plains, endless, where souls are calm:
they are my home: Mongolia, full-souled and fine.

Endless Khalkha between ranges and sandplains:
childhood-ridden endless land:
purebright ranges flicked with wolf and deer:
brightest valleys where horses thudder:
they are my home: Mongolia, full-souled and fine.

Purebright grass, high-hushing in the wind:
and plains, endless, mirage-ridden:
rocks and still stone-shadows where men met:
stone-stacked ovus where men met god and ancestors:
they are my home: Mongolia, full-souled and fine.

Grass-crowded plains, purebright and endless,
ridden endlessly in childhood and now:
flicked with free men, season and season:
life-earthed plains where five grains grow:
they are my home: Mongolia, full-souled and fine.

Awe-rearing heights – graves where ancestors are cradled:
child-flicked and ridden with free men:
endless plains where five animals grow:
life earthed with Mongol souls, on and on:
they are my home: Mongolia, full-souled and fine.

Endless, broad, deep – white-wintered:
crowded with iceglittered grass:
endless, deep, broad – bloomed with summer:
pure-sprung with songbirds from the south:
they are my home: Mongolia, full-souled and fine.

Earth living, living between Altai and Khingan:
earth kept living – passed here from my parents
to me, earth hush-grown under the sun:
to me, earth hush-glittered under the moon:
they are my home: Mongolia, full-souled and fine.

Earth of ancestors: mine, from Hun and Sung:
awe-rearing earth, shuddered by Blue Mongols:
earth made ours from the first time-tick:
earth flicked with a flag of new hope:
it's my home: Mongolia, full-souled and fine.

My country, child-ridden, grown with me:
loved, untresspassed, with me – my home:
grown, grown before and after me:
and grown now, with me: always newer and more fine:
it's my home: Mongolia, full-souled and fine.

Anonymous

In Time

Hot night hangs on the roof
like inkish sheets. All the sky
is one slept thing: and all
the air is nothing.

We sit, friends and I,
in bland electric light
bound by fretted shutters
and glass-becalmed.

Quiet. Still. The yellow
dish-steam climbs itself
in floated heaviness.
The clock is dead.

The great river runs
drop by drop by drop:
and touch by touch by touch
the camel goes into the couscous.

José Craveirinha (*b.* 1922)

3D

In the loco ...
the machine-god,
cap and boilersuit,
holds the pistons' mystery in his hand.

In the Pullman ...
the First-Class god
mellows projects in conditioned air.

And down the side-line ...
– feet braced on carriage-steel –
lung-busting,
the trolley-god.

Anonymous

Lullaby

on the moon's round cay
a gold hare squats, half-eyed …
sleep …
sleep …

an old bone man mashes rice,
look, on the moon's round cay …
sleep …
sleep …

they might be golden shows,
Nat's soft half-shades …
sleep …
sleep …

sundown's running paint,
to hush and shut your eyes …
sleep …
sleep …

NAMIBIA

Anonymous

I have to go ...

I have to go
into
the tangled
rushed
cross-strings
of hurry
and men.

You have to go
into
the tangled
rushed
cross-strings
of hurry
and men.

In this
busy-ness
you and I
will come upon
each other.
Only mountains
never meet.

Anonymous

Arere, Eiroworowin & Eomakan

By a breathless cay
held hot in heaven's arms
the man Arere lived
with his wife Eiroworowin
and their 10 puppy-happy children.

One day, like every day,
a hot, wet day, Arere padded off
to fish the breathless cay
and Eiroworowin sat
skinning in the door.

Arere padded home,
one lapis fish goggling on his stick,
and went inside. 1 2 3 4 5 6 7 8 9.
'One of the children has gone.'
'Eomakan came,' said his wife.
The day still hot in heaven's arms.

Another day, like every day,
a hot, wet day, Arere padded off
to fish the breathless cay
and Eiroworowin sat
skinning in the door.

Arere padded home,
two lapis fish goggling on his stick,
and went inside. 1 2 3 4 5 6 7 8.
'Another child has gone.'
'Eomakan came,' said his wife.
The day more hot in heaven's arms.

Every day, like every day,
a hot, wet day, Arere padded off
to fish the breathless cay
and Eiroworowin sat
skinning in the door.

Arere padded home,
more lapis fish goggling on his stick,
and went inside. 7 6 5 4 3 2 1.
'Another child has gone.'
'Eomakan came,' said his wife.
Every day hotter in heaven's arms.

One day, like every day,
a hot, wet day, Arere padded off
and hid behind a prickled bush.
Rain nailed down on his grass hat.
He waited for Eomakan to come.

The shellsand shook. Shining with rain,
Eomakan stamped along the breathless cay.
'Eiroworowin! Where's Arere?'
'Fishing the lapis fish,' she said.
'Chuck me your child
or I'll come in and eat your everything!'

But Eiroworowin sat
skinning in the door.
Eomakan stamped inside
and felt the hot, wet air
with his creamy fingers.

Arere padded in behind
and chucked a raindropped net
around his childhot head.
Eiroworowin cut his windpipe with shells.
The day on fire in heaven's arms.

By the breathless cay
Eiroworowin sat
skinning in the door.
Arere laid the lapis fish
around the more nutritious meat
for stew. The rain came down.

Iswar Ballav (*b.* 1937)

Stride On

Look skywards, but not always:
look earthwards, often.

Earth loves man, rootedly:
add the addless stars –
that many raindrops land
here; that many shoots spawn
here. Sound the soundless horizon –
that far, that far out men and men stride in.
Somewhere the rushlight lights, lights;
somewhere the rushlight pitches out, out:
men and men stride on, on.

Frederick Willem van Eeden Jr (1860–1932)

City Evening

The great uttering of the city is hushed
and the nightwind that slides through my window
brings a blurry, odd hum
like the mutter of sleeping houses.

The mantle, soft-hummed and still,
burns its nightlong thoughts:
I stare at the sheer light,
the cat butts my hands.

I think about far-passed days
when my heart started with sunshine;
when limetrees prickled me with scent;
when daffodils churned in the wind.

Where did I first find the rose,
near-white, that grows where sandbanks end? –
The cat plays on the windowsill,
rustling the curtains with its claws.

Look – flowers and sedge on my carpet, on my book;
a hawthorn blooms in the corner, in my room.
Look – faintred roses and shut lilacs
wrap in my rings …

A shadow slides in and everything lours away –
the cat watches at the window,
drowned in darkness;
its tail thumps.
Now chill, black thoughts
roll in from the black city,
climb out of the chill, dark canals,
rippling-wet.

They glide, hushblack, through the window,
one for each shoulder, one for my head,
one for my chest, one for each temple,
settling, pressing, cramping, gagging.

The blurry, odd noise;
the nightwind's lap and burr;
the houses' stricken dreams;
the mantle hums its thoughts.

Anonymous

Treeback

Birds fan, grubs snout
the tree
Rata
smack-axed
down.

Birds fan, grubs snout:
hish hish
the jammed leaves:
clitter clitter
the axed-out skelfs.

Birds fan, grubs snout:
the branches
uncrash –
grack grack –
back out, rearmed.

Birds fan, grubs snout:
the leaves
outlever,
sheeek sheeek,
flicker-flags again.

Birds fan, grubs snout:
the bits and switches
shiver, creak, close, fit,
zip zip,
unfelling.

Birds fan, grubs snout:
the branches outspread –
and up *grrroooo*
and up *ggrrrrrrooooooooo*
the tree bellows straight!

Ruben Dario (1867–1916)

Tropic Afternoon

This afternoon is grey and sad.
The sea sheets itself in velvet
and the sky sheets itself
in aching space.

Bitter, looming drums
roll out of its black room:
when the wind frets,
the waves squall.

Seamist-fiddles
play the dimming sun:
white spume plays one note –
a hopeless one.

Their music sogs the sky;
and the wind runs on and on,
carrying the sad, long song
of the sea.

The skyline's brasshorn
blares its knotted symphony
like the shaking voice
of a mountain:

like something invisible …
like the rasped note
that weaves the wind with
a lion.

Anonymous

The Mouse

We stretch under a black, starred sky.
The fired snapsticks crackle.

The world, unlit and wide,
gutters down fields of stubble.

The moon is gone tonight.
Somewhere. Somewhere else.

We stretch under a black, starred sky.
The cut stalks rattle.

The world is dark and wide.
A mouse scoots into the fire.

The moon is gone tonight.
Something hurts more than flames.

Anonymous

Bloom-Girl

now
you are
a mirror
that the sun
should never
see
a lamb
that the leafdrip
should never
touch
a breath
wound with
hair
a rushlight
that men
see looking
by
a moon
that men
see hoping
by
a kite-feather
that one man
will
wear
a straight line
drawn
by
God.

Kali Kolsson (*d.* 1158)

Two Poems

1

I have nine principal talents:
I am virtually unbeatable at chess,
I read runes faultlessly with a few insignificant exceptions,
I may frequently be found reading or creating beautiful things,
I can ski,
I am an excellent shot, I can row tolerably,
and I am cognisant of the arts
of performing on the harp and declaiming poetry.

2

For five loathsome weeks
we have been stumping in the mud.
Grimsby is the filthiest place
I have ever had the misfortune of shopping in.
Now we are whistling across the seagulls' moorland
in our Beaked Elk,
over the waves to Bergen,
thank goodness.

Anonymous

truth

breast
nursery
school
university
books
paper
talks
of thought:

it's good
to know
the truth:

but it's better
to talk
about
palmtrees.

Allama Mohammed Iqbal (1875–1938)

Poem

Are you Alive, Dead or DeadAlive?
Call These Three Witnesses – and judge.

One: call Consciousness, Your Own.
Quiz yourself with your own light.

Two: call Consciousness, An Other's.
Quiz yourself with another's light.

Three: call Consciousness, God's.
Quiz yourself with God's light.

Think: you are Alive and Forever.
As Alive and Forever as God.

Think: as Alive and Forever as God
when you dare, and see his face.

Think: what is Going-To-Heaven?
A hunt for a witness to your Aliveness.

Think: whose evidence makes you Forever,
Alive and Forever as God?

Can you stand, unquaked, in His hereness?
When you dare you are gold, pure gold.

Are you only a dab of dust?
Pull your life-knot tight –

hold your speck-self tight –
and blaze it gold and Alive.

Call Alive to the stand of the Sun!
Rewhittle old dead-habited You

and be new. Judge that Alive.
Or you are a smoke-ring, wasting, wasting.

Anonymous

The Bungle-man

the bungle-man
thinks
with crewless brains:
like the boat-bob
from Ngerechemai
who tagged
the where-is
of his fishtraps
with a cloud.

Anonymous

Young once ...

Young once
and dreaming,
back up to a tree;
yellow, and a stick
poking at stones;
sleepy at midday,
gummed up and telling me –

I know love
when it passes:
smell it
when it passes.

Take her tender, green and new,
like the eating-yucca:
sweet and zested,
balmy-soft
and sugar-raw,
ah!

His eyeballs glittered
at the sun
and while I passed
I said –

Wisdom is the name
of disappointment
with old men,
who call it that
to dignify
their age.

And midday called me;
and he slept.

Dus Mapun

O Myland Woman

Papua-woman
Buka-woman
NewGuinea-woman
Upland-woman
Oh myland woman I feel sad sad for you

You see Mr Australia driving round in his car
You see Mr America driving round in his truck
You see Mr England riding round on his motorbike
You see Mr New Zealand riding round on his bicycle
and you stand up, and look, look, and you shake, shake.
Oh myland woman I feel sad sad for you

You see Mr Papua flapping past on foot
You see Mr Buka slapping past on foot
You see Mr NewGuinea trekking round on foot
You see Mr Upland plodding round on foot
You hear the blackman say *Morning myland woman*
You turn away and say *Brazen brazen*
Oh myland woman I feel sad sad for you

Oh myland woman
before your mouth was brown
and now your mouth is red
before your hair was puff-loose
and now your hair is yanked tight
before your breasts lay soft and cool
and now your breasts poke hard and hemmed
You look look in the mirror and say
Twenty dollars twenty dollars good time
Oh myland woman I feel sad sad for you

Old Mr England says Ah *come to me ah*
Young Mr Australia sees you and says
Ah black beautiful gorgeous
I'll make you the queen of heaven
You listen and you think it's true
Oh myland woman I feel sad sad for you

I stand here I watch it all
I sit here I think think
Oh myskin woman I feel sad sad for you
Oh myland woman I feel very sad sad for you

Herib Campos Cervera (1905–1953)

Sent

Brother:
I'll look for you in the back of corners.
And you won't be there.

I'll look for you in a bird-cloud.
And you won't be there.

I'll look for you in a beggar's hand.
And you won't be there.

And I'll look for you
in the gold-picked page of an Hourbook.
And you won't be there.

I'll look for you in the gnomes' night.
And you won't be there.

I'll look for you in the plunk of a musicbox.
And you won't be there.

(I'll look for you in Children's eyes.
And you'll be there.)

Gonzalez Prada (1848–1918)

Forced Labour

Okay son – I'm going.
Morning gongs the volcano.
Hand me my walkingstick
and my jaguarsandals.

Here's your sandals, dad,
and here's your walkingstick.
Why are you looking at me and crying?
Tell me where you're going.

The Whites' wicked laws
drag me out of my house.
I'm going to work and hunger, son:
I'm going to the deadly mine.

Tell me before you go, dad –
tell me when you'll come back.
When the upland llama, son,
loves the desert sand.

Anonymous

People tell me ...

People tell me not
to rattle you for love:
they say you miss
some means in me.

People tell me not
to flutter love and tenderkind:
I say my unbacked love
is dearer than gold.

My love for you is spendless,
endless, mendless:
I am your rich company
and broke without you.

And if you doubt
that Love is Me entirely –
keep me alive merely,
who means to love you.

Maria Pawlikowska-Jasnorzewska (1895–1945)

Polish Colours

White – bloodred.
Bloodred linen – white linen.
Flag-bandage
that dammed the bled soak.
The wind unfurls this ledger of a wound,
lifts the heroic swab,
keepsake,
debt
and dictum.

Fernando Pessoa (1888–1935)

My smalltown bell ...

My smalltown bell,
blue-voiced on the still evening –
each burst chime
rings in my soul.

And your chiming so slow –
and aching with life:
even the first chime
rings like a chime again.

You chime at me close
when I pass, always unstill:
but you are a dream
chiming distance in my soul.

And with every chime
that rings into the high sky,
I feel the past draw back,
and longing draw near.

Anonymous

Unspent

I feel sick.
I grab my wallet
and drive into Doha.
I shop for a pair
of bright black shoes.

I feel sick.
I grab my chequebook
and drive into Doha.
I buy a box
of glittered macaroons.

I feel sick.
I grab my creditcard
and drive into Doha.
I get a hundred bloodroses
and a packet of painkillers.

I still feel sick.
I grab my spend-keen heart
and drive into Doha.
I go to the chemist's
but they don't sell *Love-Me*.

Ion Minulescu (1881–1944)

Mechanical-landscape-poem

Vacuous monochrome of a watery day,
damping the galled blues of a homewards goodstrain
that squeals cheek out of three bronchitic valves,
and climbs a slope out of fatalistic flats that die on the harp
of funeral-parlours.
With a beeswax-spill scent,
elusive incense-oose,
Eau de Cologne
and lilies.

In the Olt Valley
or the interminable Prahova Valley …
the same
watery-day-landscape everywhere.
Every goodstrain limns
the same ordinary blues
while it tugs at the takeoff of
Expresstrains that climb a slope with the grace of an aeroplane! …
The same insipid blues
the same trio-squeal
clamouring for morning-mercy
and boring the passengers.

Green monochrome:
cardboard hills and trees –
vacuous spoof of exhausted animals –
that climb Calvary again with every train and road.
Travesty of ideas and slave-imagination …

Mechanical-landscape-poem –
aspiration
of new art
and science –
Cezanne would paint you some other way,
but I see you like that.

Nikolai Gumilev (1886–1921)

The Worker

A grizzly squab comrade
stumps up and down sweating
at the mouth of a howling blastfurnace.

His hot tomato eyelids
blink at his reliable eyes,
still willingly at work.

His scorched comrades have all gone.
But he stays to cast the bullet
that will kill me.

Finished. His scarlet eyes swim and smile.
He stumps home in the wide white moonlight
to his wife and a strawfizzing bed.

The bullet will spit squealing
across the soapy Dvina
goring a hole through my past.

I will fall biting the air
and burst. And the dust will drain
my soft cherry blood.

And God will repay me forever and forever
for my short dark unjust life.
The old squab worker in a grey suit did this.

Anonymous

Visitors

At my uncle's
door
just beside
the chickenwire
I spy a
woodbag

full with a

loud mitten
rude cane
egotistical slipper
bad-tempered umbrella
pessimistic duster
harebrained poncho
miserable scarf
stuckup flipflop
moaning beret
giggly billycock
shy gumboot

and inside
I find
eleven
admirable
men.

Anonymous

Safe, here, now...

Safe, here, now,
your dipstroke journey done,
your seawake hushed
in the unbubbled tide,
skerries, reefs and straits
coasted, crossed and shot –
now, safe, here,
we meet.

Welcome.

Safe, here, now,
your dragstroke journey halfdone,
your seawake unmade
in the unbubbled tide,
skerries, reefs and straits
to coast, cross and shoot
when we part
and you strike for home.

Anonymous

The Death of Saint Marinus

The whole man flies,
flat out on his mountaintop.
Clouds touch him
like silver rags.
Down below, his little, won land,
like a shoe on a stone leg,
walks out of usage.

He says:
I leave you freedom
from other men.

Wind bellies his stone cell
like a rock-sail, and he
and his little All
disconnect, driven and done.
Down below, his little, won land,
like the hem on a stone coat,
sweeps out of usage.

He said:
I leave you freedom
from other men.

Alda do Espirito Santo (*b.* 1926)

To Tania

night warmed by an african moon
streets mottled by shadows
I reach thirsty
for our vast mother africa
and hoist my unwordly song for you
and ask earth to hold
your taken roads
your vast lifeline
all drawn along your self
for your self
our roads made plain
all specks and thankless sadness
brushed off for you
long song of our
great mother africa

Anonymous (13th–14th Century)

Tie up my bones ...

Tie up my bones and walk them away
with the whitenap camels
wherever they ship their skeps.

Dig me down somewhere on the road,
brother and custom-straight,
as if it was me with yours.

Lug me up out of the greengrape thickets
to a high hill and fix me a view
that will sometimes have you.

Yell your name when you blow past
with the whitenap camels
and my bones will brighten.

Fast like we did in our breathless days,
brother and custom-straight.
I am fasting and breathless now.

At the hot rerise of bones
we will find each other in the dust
and wolf happiness.

Anonymous

The piddling ant has its bibble of gall …

The piddling ant has its bibble of gall:
tanquam, the unpleasant, stabby Prickleback has its fin-pins.
The shrubbiest tree has its bashful shrivel-berry.
The wren has flappers *quantuluscumque* to fly with whacking birds.
The bee has a song, howsomever its buzz-bore droning
does not, I admit, compare with the blackbird's.
Flint is a Stone of the Stone Family *etsi*
it is not as cream-and-polish-pretty as the pearl.
And Mantua is not half so greatly gorgeous
as Rome, *quamquam* they are both towns.
Little randans ply the seashuttle with Golden Galleons
and pennies buy pleasant-pleasing pleasures as well as pounds.
Gutters have runlets *tamquam* great-glide rivers roil and roll:
and love is love with Harry and Your Highness.

Malick Fall (1920–1978)

Nightstart

My little towns are scared of the dark
But the dark nudges them
Before it wraps them in black

A mother rereds the dim smoulder
A child taps home the goats
A father thanks the hangback black
And night nips a wisp of the little town
So kindly, fright dims itself away

Good night, little African towns

Anonymous

Sea-palms

Each steamy night
in the dank, dark,
stream-sticky gully,
the mantree,
its brown penis,
stretching hard,
attended by a
glittered clag of insects,
rumble-stretches at
the rumble-stretching
womantree, whose
vegetable gulch,
attended by a slap
of little black parrots,
comes wetly
rumble-nearer, nearer ...

Way above the
busy, pillared trunks,
the stiff-spread claws
of their hair-fans
rattle like a thousand
excited wooden hearts,
and hide their
giant, squidging,
elephant-rumbling
rabbet
from the moon,
who blanches
with imagination
while men
sweat through
bad dreams.

Anonymous

Careful!

pull
a
rope
and
the
rope
pulls
in
the
forest
and
with
the
forest
leopards
come
to
town.

S.N. Masuri (*b.* 1927)

Day's End

Day's end. Robins tweep,
coolly rocking my mood.
And the calm world dislights
to take up its night.

Now, suddenly, all, silence –
whose slipping time disquiets my soul.
Left adrift, high-dry, it feels
the hour-tide ebb, dark, away.

I think of the perfect span
of earth's bright colours
in the height of day: and a
light-souled happiness calms me back.

And the breeze-sway calms me back,
bringing the muezzin's lovesong,
that calls me to the soul's thoughts
of great God, and all my thanks.

Jan Smrek (1898–1982)

December

God gave a sign – and the
quibbleless, brainblessed angels
tugged the clouds' featherbed
(where the saints were oversleeping):
and when we went out
snowy feathers were falling.

We are tickled: because
we can't duck the feathers.
And in the park – look –
no greentrees – everything
white, whitewhitewhite –
oh
and the church roofs
and the belltowers
and the girls swanning down the streets
all fluffed up
and red-lipped
like May
and walking, all walking,
and the trams empty.

And the women walk, looks-proud,
all walking, light, unpressed,
luminous and eased
with beauty:
and their neat heads sink
like soft roses on their
snowmen's coatchests
and snow falls on
the city
like a heap of white bouquets.

Laughter and buzz brim
in the evening white-spread square,
and the people
crackle in crowds
and sudden passes.
And along the river,
here and there,
wrapped up in night and white,
two by two they miss the path,
looking in each other's eyes instead.

We won't disturb them,
embarrass them: we'll slip by
in snowy silence.

Down the white street,
a shoe-stamped path,
lightblock houses and
open gates,
and glowed windows gleaming
a warm breath
through glass-iced flowers:
and a sweet tumble of steam
from the samovar.

France Preseren (1800–1849)

Where?

I bite my nails. I prowl round, here – there –
Friends say – Where are you going?

Hah! Ask a cloud in the sky,
ask a wave in the sea

blasted round and round with storms,
dictator-driven.

They don't know: the cloud, the waves –
and I: pushed round by despair – somewhere.

What I know is she's gone.
Lost. Forever. Ah, hopeless, hopeless.

There's nowhere anywhere
where I can unfind my hell.

Celo Kalagoe (*d.* 2001)

This johnny ...

This johnny
is Mr Strong from Strongtown.
He's got the government by the whatsits
He's got the prime minister by the whatsits
because he's the johnny
that runs the Big Men
he's the johnny that runs them round.
He opens all the Big Men's mouths
and they all talk Mr Strong talk
He candycakes all the Big Men's tongues
and they all talk Mr Sweet talk
He unshuts all the Big Men's eyes
and they all see Mr Strong's Progress Highway Go Now!

This johnny
is a friend of mine
Mm he wears all the gear
and all the flash jangles that go with the gear
But he's got me by the whatsits too
He's got me running all over the show too
oh looking for work work work
and working working working working
till I'm just a bunch of bones Ah

This johnny
is Mr Dollar.

Anonymous

Camel

Camel. When your footthuds flag,
whose leaden lifts outdrain you –
Ah camel. When your sheeny sides matt
all ashy like a thorn-arm –
My camel. When your up-lofted neck slumps
sapped and thin as a straw –
Ah camel. When your mouth seres,
o-ed with the dust of death –
Camel. When the sky stops shifting colours –
then the land is a bareburnt blank.

Eugene Marais (1871–1936)

Dance of Sister Rain

Our Sister's dance!
She eyes us, breezy, round the pike-top,
shy eyes,
hush chuckles:
and way away she asks with a hand –
her armloops glitter, beads blink –
she asks quietly,

asks the winds,
asks them to the raindance:
the clear land looks long, and the wedding wild.

Antelope thunder off the flats,
crowd at the hilltops,
snouts pumping,
gulping the wind,
craning down at her light spoors in the dust.

The weemen way underground hear her feet pat past,
climb closer, and sing, little-voiced –
Sister, Sister: you're here, you're here.

Her beads rattle,
her legloops glint copper in the sun's spin.
The eagle's fire-feather sheets on her head:
she walks down from the pike-tops,
folds out the grey blanket both-arms-wide:
and the wind's breath breaks.
Our Sister's dance!

Frederico García Lorca (1898–1936)

Song of the Sterile Orange Tree

Axeman.
Cut down my shade.
Free me from the gall
of fruitless sight.

Why born in the air of mirrors?
Day winds close round and round me;
night spawns me
in all its cold stars.

Let me live blind to me,
and dream that
ants and buzzards
are my greenness and my birds.

Axeman.
Cut down my shade.
Free me from the gall
of fruitless sight.

Anonymous

The Hunters Ask God

Indigolava Kirri-Amma.
Eat this, drink that. And deal us our Enough.
Pay us our hunted-meat.
Whoa! the Elephant, whom we would rather not meet.
Whoa! the Bear, whom we would rather not meet.
Whoa! the Leopard, whom we would rather not meet.
Push Enough Pangolin our way please.
Push Enough Iguana our way please.
Push Enough Monkeys our way please.
We would like to meet the Sambhur-deer if you don't mind.
We would like to meet the Pig if you don't mind.
Oh, all-the-way-there and all-the-way-back,
look after us, and deal us our Enough.
Indigolava Kirri-Amma.

Anonymous

makeme

the
the
the
he
he
his
monkey
arsehole
higher
more
climbs
goes
shows

Anonymous

sea

masts – loose paddles – hulls –
clack and rattle –
lemon-lit – and sunrise
shines the fishboats'
insect oars
pricking at the sealine –
burst with light –
the sky behind
a yellow door –
and smaller still –
and smaller still –

and day stands
like the unstirred air
inside a house –

midday – and the sea
lies alone
straight as a
window-ledge –
straight as a
swept floor –

evening – and the sky
reds alone –
full as a
window-blind –
full as a
wood wall –

masts – loose paddles – hulls –
clack and rattle –
the land waits for
the insect-boats –
the sea has no
back door –

Anonymous

the monkey knows ...

the monkey knows
what tree to climb
not the one in the hat
not the one that goes up
on the beach like a yawn
not the ones that are wired
in a hot humming line
not the one with the leaves
made out of men's shirts
not the one with a bald
yellow ball for a crown
not the one with two trunks
and the branches between
not the one with one leaf
and a big brass band
not the one on the roof
not the one by the pool
not the one that lights up
by itself in the night
or the one that says God
or the one that says Drink
but the one with the view
of the roll of the sea
and the bed of bright leaves
and the near peeled fruit
the one where the ages
of fathers and grandfathers
grinned and grew old

Anonymous

loveshock

Ah Ajaak Ajaak
Ajaak
mine when she blubbed in a pouch
Ajaak
mine when she lambly first danced
Ajaak
mine when she spelled first-loveliness
Ah Ajaak Ajaak

and she grew to it all
and another man stole it

Ah Ajaak Ajaak

think of me though you don't
punch-hearted snap-lifed

Ah Ajaak Ajaak
Ajaak
God runs me through with you
Ajaak
Maraang runs me through with you
Ajaak
I wreck for Kaat Ateem's girl
Ah Ajaak Ajaak

and I blub for her lamb loveliness
and Ajaak is gone

Ah Ajaak Ajaak

Anonymous

I want a heart ...

I want a heart that fits me,
and furnished with a soul,
a spark, some need, two lives, and love,
or else no heart at all.

I want two shoes that fit me,
and furnished with a sole,
a rolling sky, some road, and hope,
or else no shoes at all.

I want a face that fits me,
and furnished with my soul,
a mirror of my heart and hope,
or else no face at all.

Anonymous

You

Back from being
with you –
the bush rustles –
empty –
the sky stands –
empty –
the wind moves –
empty

Back from being
with you –
my heart –
empty –
my words –
empty –
my house –
empty

Back from being
with you –
I remember –
something –
I think up –
something –
I see –
something

My grassthatch –
your hair –
my windows –
your eyes –
my door –
your mouth –
my land –
your otherwise

Back from being
with you –
the bush –
your words –
the sky –
your beauty –
the wind –
your thoughts

Back from being
with you –
my heart –
yours –
my words –
yours –
my house –
you

Back from being
with you –
I remember –
words –
I think up –
thoughts –
I see –
beauty

Karin Boyes (1900–1941)

That profound waiting time …

That profound waiting time
before leaf and budbreak:
trees shudder, near their bursting gaud
as purple birch and limelit aspen,
and creeks well, sunred.
That unseen things' show-time:
when all earth is a stripped, brimming womb,
the spirit juddering tongues,
and twilight, too, prods and overdoes,
like unstopped love.
The world winds up to spring,
now, before the end of hope:
in the greenest woods,
the raringest stuff;
and trees and men sleep-mumble,
'Ah, we wanted more.'

Conrad Meyer (1825–1898)

Blackshadow Chestnut

Blackshadow chestnut:
my breeze-blown summer tent,
who stoops its heavy branches
in the lake edge, whose leaves
are thirsty, and drink:
blackshadow chestnut.

Children splash in the harbour-bay
with happy yells and squabbles,
and swim, white-shining,
amongst the braid
of its leaf-weave:
blackshadow chestnut.

And the shoreside, and the lake
lour, and the late ferry burbles by –
and a flash sheens
from its red shiplamp,
ripples like fitful writing
on the water's low roll … ripples
until the strange flame-script
flickers out
under its branches:
blackshadow chestnut.

Maisun bint Bahdal (*d.* 700)

Give me ... I'll give you ...

Give me a hurly house: I'll give you this echo-high Hall.
Give me a bum-calling dog: I'll give you this miaow-mogul.
Give me a snug shirt: I'll give you this tussah seige.
Give me homey crumbs: I'll give you this cold bloomer.
Give me windtalk in wall-gaps: I'll give you this binging bell-drum.
Give me my straight-shaped cousin: I'll give you these fat emmets.
Give me my plain hard hicks: I'll give you these ripe bloodcushions.
Give me my field-fed house, honoured in the grass.

Anonymous

My horse thickens ...

My horse
thickens,
thudder-strong.

At night
I bump him
extra hay.

My hot money
multiplies,
bullion-bright.

At night
I hurry round
my second job.

Ferdowsi (935–1025)

I've worked so hard ...

I've worked, I've worked so hard; reading, reading,
so much to know, arabic, persian, so much to find,
so much to collect, stories from here, stories from there:
now – ah, sixty, sixty years have gone –
and my young days have keeled
into disappointment and wrong:
and I parrot with soft sadness
my copy of Bu Tahir Kousrawani:
The story of Youth is short:
I hardly remember it. Now
I long to read it again.
But the thin bright book is shut.

Anonymous

The Ten-Day Visitor

Yay! A Visitor! Day one.
Dish him up rice and coconut
in a coconut hull.
Welcome, Mr Visitor!

Yay! A Visitor! Day two.
Butter him up with milk and ghee.
If Mr Visitor behaves himself,
oblige Mr Visitor!

Whoh! A Visitor! Day three.
Nothing left. Well,
just three pinchy helpings
warmed up for Mr Visitor!

Whoh! A Visitor! Day four.
Hand him a hoe.
This is an hoblique hint –
Go Home, Mr Visitor!

Hm. A Visitor. Day five.
He's skinny as a needle.
Everyone's whispering and pretending not to.
Mr Visitor is making snorting noises.

Hm. A Visitor. Day six.
Everyone's hogging scraps and pretending not to.
Everyone's lurking in nooks,
hiding from Mr Visitor!

Gawd. A Visitor. Day seven.
Mr Visitor is a bloody pain.
If the roof catches fire,
blame Mr Visitor!

Gawd. A Visitor. Day eight.
Please come and say goodbye!
If you see him take one bloody step outside
yell at him 'Bye!' 'Seeya!' 'Go home, Mr Visitor!'

Booo! A Visitor! Day nine.
Please go away forever, Mr Visitor.
Please don't ever pass this way again!
Please, Mr Visitor, don't ever come back!

Booo! A Visitor! Day ten.
Guess who: kick kick, slap slap,
punch punch. Get him out of here!
Haha! It's Mr Visitor!

Anonymous

Goodland

This place, these bounds,
this space, these grounds,
this state, these lands –
long-eyeful-of-peace;
teeming ease.

Where water
is fish
are:
where fields
are rice
is.

King This, King That,
time-giants,
golden hills,
mis-
employ
no man.

The businessman does business
if he likes.
Or blossoms
another way.

This place, these bounds,
this space, these grounds;
this state, these lands –
its people blossom,
their faces
happy-glowed.

Anonymous

Night Roof

The night roof is a right-round city,
lightpricked with men and wild things:
but, there, no man
has ever killed a chook or goat,
no bear has ever wiped its game:
no crashes, no slips.
Everything still-lives.

Anonymous

The Story of Kepa Falekaono

Tukuaho: what a bastard.
Two years of him in
the Big Seat is more
than enough
in my opinion,
said Tupouniua,
I'll bash his head
in.

Plan: kill the bastard.
I'll do it when he's
asleep, said Tupouniua.
How, said Finau
Ulukalala, *will you*
know it's him?
Because twenty people
slept there.

Clever: by the bastard's smell.
Every night, said
Tupouniua, *he's rubbed*
all over with
coconut-seaweed-
blossom-blubber-oil
so I can find the
bastard in the dark

The right night: the bastard's house.
Tupouniua tiptoed into
Mu'a and the bastard's house
swinging a head-bashing
club. *Sniff sniff*, he went,
sniff sniff, right up to the smell
of coconut-seaweed-
blossom-blubber-oil.

BASH: bash bash the bastard.
Tupouniua did. And a voice
said, *Who's that? Who dares
disturb the sleep of
Tukuaho?* Ah. Wrong
man, so Tupouniua
bashed the brains out of
Tukuaho again.

What?: had happened?
Kepa Falekaono had happened.
Tukuaho's blubber-rubber.
Tupouniua's friend.
What did he think?
1. warn Tukuaho: Tupouniua dies.
2. don't warn Tukuaho: Tukuaho dies.
3. Think of something else.

Something else: sweet sacrifice.
Tukuaho fell asleep.
Kepa Falekaono rubbed himself
with the coconut-seaweed-
blossom-blubber-oil
and lay down
beside Tukuaho
who was snoring happily.

How did he feel: waiting?
Hearing Tupouniua tiptoe into
Mu'a and Tukuaho's house?
And sniffing, sniffing, nearer,
nearer, his head-bashing
club swinging?
Sniff sniff – waiting –
BASH!

Dead: we can feel your pain.
Sweet Kepa Falekaono,
killed in the house
of Tukuaho by your
friend. A brave idea
though it didn't work.
Sweet sacrifice.
Deathless honour.

Anonymous

Silk Cotton Tree

Work's finished
and I'm going home.

Come with me, Louey,
work's finished
and I'm going home.
The sky's not so light now.

The wind rattles the grass,
come with me, Louey,
work's finished
and I'm going home.

Come with me, Louey,
I'm going home,
just past the rapping shed
there's the Silk Cotton Tree.
The sky's not so light now.

Work's finished.
Come with me, Louey,
the wind strokes its silky hair
and rattles its skull-bones.
Come with me, Louey,
I'm going home.

Work's finished
and I'm going home.
There's eyes between the branches.
Come with me, Louey,
the sky's not so light now.

Come with me, Louey,
I'm going home.
There's hair like a hundred beards
and chattering twig-teeth.
Work's finished,
come with me, Louey,
I'm going home.

Come with me, Louey,
the wind rattles the grass.
There's a big wisp-heaving head
that gobbles the wind.
It's not so light now.
Come with me, Louey,
I'm going home.

Work's finished.
It's not so light now.
Come with me, Louey,
I'm going home,
past the rapping shed
and the Silk Cotton Tree,
come with me, Louey,
I'm going home.

Albert Memmi (*b*. 1920)

a shot of sunlight lasts just too long …

a shot of sunlight
lasts just too long
and it's dogdays

an eye of water
flutters in a bucket
and it's the uncut sea

a blue door
at a turn in the road
and it's the deep deep skyworks

a quoit of peppers
on a dust-falling wall
and it's my bloodtapped heart

Ahmet Hasim (1884–1933)

Moonstruck Storks

Milkymoonstruck, a cool disposition of storks
contemplate a pool in still council.

The sky is a hungup lagoon tonight, deep-high,
and pricked with a million bluecooped gnats.

What are the birds that fish up there, and sip
the airy, crackled bugs with glittered wakes?

The storks contemplate such questions in a still council ...
moonstruck ... at the pool ... into the night ...

Anonymous

Pick a pomegranate ...

Pick a pomegranate.
Its fiery wooden skin:
its seeming burst.
Try it:
and cold, cinnabar
eyes seem
their own fire.
And no smell.

Pick a friend.
His fiery willow front:
his seeming burst.
Try him:
and cold, windy
words seem
their own fire.
And no proof.

TUVALU

Anonymous

I wish ...

I wish I was
a dragonfly
hallelujah
in sungleam.

Okot p'Bitek (1931–1982)

The Eyeshop

Where's
the Eyeshop?
When will I ever see Ms Right?
I ogle her with anger.

Vasyl Symonenko (1935–1963)

Lonely

Often I'm lonely – some Crusoe
looking for ships unsettling the horizon.
Thinking drowns feebly
in a sticky bladderwrack of words.
I puncture the bluesky
with razor-eyes;
I'm wrapped in pelts
of shot hopes.
– O, my Friday, where are you!
Broadsides of hopelessness rip out of my throat,
cracking away through careless distance:
– Deliver me, O God, some enemy,
if you deny me a friend!

Anonymous

A B C D

A doesnt know
he doesnt know
so A is thick
keep away

B knows
he doesnt know
so B is green
teach him something

C doesnt know
he knows
so C is dreamy
wake him up

D knows
he knows
so D is bright
ask him over

Julio Herrera y Reissig (1875–1910)

Siesta

Just one clock dings … the shy bell
that counts the town's contented boredom …
its sour gleam in the January sun …
like the faraway look of a crabbit old-timer …

the chemist sits snoozing in his doorway …
a hen chooks in the shush-still square …
and a priest studies the air … and his prayerbook …
by the fire … slowburning bluebeech branches …

every house is hushed … a harshless sky
makes work holy … divides chores …
mothers, sisters, aunts, washing clothes …
croon softly … in a ring …

workers' clothes … stiff-fit on Sunday …
and the moseying donkey clips on the pavement …
and clatters away … kicking the local mutts …

Paiute Song

like always ...

like always
like forever
snow holds
the hills
the deer
the high-horn
stalk down
tracking
the south-sun
wattlebeans
and clumpgrass
thunder-drums
blast in
the hill-tents
like always
like forever
we snap
sage-seeds
dry deer-meat
summer-skinned
sick of
our squats
our smoke-stenched
shirts
sick for
the south-sun
and limber
hillgrass.

Rauf Parfi (*b.* 1943)

Today I dreamed all day ...

Today I dreamed all day. I dreamed
I drove round Bukhara. I dreamed
dizzy minarets, I dreamed
rosegardens skimmed my shoes.
I dreamed I drove round Bukhara.
I dreamed the Sun came with me
and thawed tangles, ran snarls:
a bluesailed stone outshining Always.
I dreamed dizzy minarets,
jealous-faced. I dreamed
History, in front of me, *flash!*
run in a skyblue flame. I dreamed
rosegardens skimmed my shoes. I dreamed
a skyblue flame running on and on ...
Bukhara, and in it a skyblue rose,
took me forever ... forever. I dreamed
it took out my senses:
I dreamed I saw my heart ...
Today I dreamed all day. I dreamed
I drove round Bukhara.

Anonymous

and then night fell

in the beginning
it was hard:

men worked all day
all day was all

always day
always work

the sun spun
unmoved afloat

hung between
heaven and earth

nothing changed
nothing moved

always day
always work

and all the crickets
lived in heaven

whirring in a silent sheen
of lemon light

and men worked
and nothing changed

all day was all
all day was all

and one day
in the one day

in the silent sheen
of heaven

a lemon man
with legs of light

picked a cricket
out of a yellow breeze

and put it carefully
in his cricket-creel

and the gold toffee
floor of heaven

creaked and cracked
cracked and crackled

with the weight
of that one more cricket

the lemon man
belonged in heaven

and while the floor
creaked and cracked

he took hold of
a shining breeze

and saved himself
a hole cracked in the floor

his legs of light
dangled in the all day

and scrambled back
to heaven

and the cricket-creel
tumbled through the sky

down and down and down
past the sun

hung between
heaven and earth

and the working men
looked up

their diggers still
in amazed arms

and watched
the cricket-creel

tumble through the sky
and bang!

they watched amazed
nothing moved nothing changed

and then
the crickets

one by one
whirring out

like flakes of light
from heaven

flickered at the
trees and grass

and sat
and sang

and something moved
something changed

the all day dimmed
the blue sky turned

grinding like
a grinding-stone

the sun rolled down
and then night fell

and the men
stopped working

and watched night fall
and hurried home

their diggers cold
in amazed arms

and sang themselves
and slept

and every day
has every night

when crickets sing
then night falls

and men stop work
and sleep.

Karol Wojtyla (*b.* 1920)

The Wall

I see a wall; but unwhole.
Wax-white pillars draw up astride the bays
where plaster Saints, stopped with life,
lean out to leave us, by one still sign – so –
and open books, the mighty Purpose blown in man.

And the vaultroof lies like a feather on it,
and men's lives like a feather, remote in their stray, tired hearts,
even earth's infinite black room lies like nothing:
it stays, stays holding these, as long as men are born, and mothers'
milk is theirs.

Vincente Gerbasi (1913–1992)

Hallucinatory Sunset, with Sons

To refind the horse
in the gloaming spinney:
to walk in its slow-water eyes
where bruised birds float:
to come to the rushes' bonfire,
the wood-pigeon's sky,
its chirr lost in the watery banks:
to see the pine-maddered hill:
to stir bamboos in a bated round
when the frog-pool glimmers:
to follow the devil's horses' bolt
round and round a water-flower:
to roll out rugs under the trees where
beggars come and sleep in the glow-worm air:
to run a puff of woolly donkeys
and follow with my sons through the blue cicadas' skywriting.

Luu Trong Lu (*b.* 1912)

Autumn End

Sometimes
do you
breathe
the buzz
we had
when we
were young …

sometimes …
when autumn redstock
lose their leaves
in my empty
dustyard …

and flutebreath
coos through
faroff curtains
down the empty
air …

sometimes
do you
think
me back …

sometimes …
when you unhitch
raw redleaves
from their branches …

sometimes
do you
think
me back …

when sparrow-churr
and wind-hoots
misknow
my heart,
flat-cold
like an autumn
lake, leaden
with night
and nothing …

I hang on
days: but you
rush them …

autumn ends,
winter runs
down the cold
riverbank
and you quickly
marry …

sometimes
do you
breathe
the buzz
we had
when we
were young …

and think
me back
sometimes …

with that summer
and its green
love
that buzzes now
in a greenyard
in my heart.

Anonymous

Silk-spread Blackbird

Silk-spread, tawn-beak,
milk-tongue blackbird,
go to Cydweli,
ask how my love is.

One, two, three things are beyond me:
telling stars in the frost,
taking my hand to the moon,
knowing my love's mind.

Anonymous

Ox

My ox is called
God's-Love.

I feed him
out of my arms.

Day by day by day.
Dutiful. Undodging.

My ox is called
God's-Love.

I feed him even now.
Out of my cripple-chair.

Broken by his
butted thanks.

Day by day by day.
Dutiful. Undone.

Oscar Davico (1909–1989)

The Cell

Cold night in a cell.
I finger the walls, sleep-waking.
Alone in blackened space,
I mew, childlost, for home.

My strength slips – to its nothing ...
please ... come ...
tell me moonshine stories
and I'll sleep to them now.

Sweet shaken boy,
I die in your darkness:
they call you killer –
I love you more.

I never killed. I fought
for free-life, for quiet,
undeath and heartrest.
And fought a good war.

I gave my deathless years
to it all: and believe.
I know the Newtime is coming –
I can see its first sun.

Anonymous

My dugout flibbles ...

My dugout flibbles
flat out down the river.
Monkeys yawl and chitter
tree by tree by tree.
Ah, what's happened,
Jungle-Boss?

The wee monkey's bust his leg
and everybody's bawling.

Ah, River-Boss,
zip that paddle
and go tell mum
her wee monkey's crying:
the wee monkey's bust his leg
and everybody's bawling.

Anonymous

Loveburn

I'm burned by love
like a fire-frayed,
heat-chewed
rope-pipe.

She smiles
a milk-white smile,
cool, close,
and I'm burned by love.

She sways
like a limber tree
over bushes,
and I'm burned by love.

I'm burned by love
like a fire-frayed,
heat-chewed
rope-pipe.

Her sugar skin
draws my mind
away from me,
and it's burned by love.

My babied heart
lies helpless in the
cot of her hands,
and I'm burned by love.

I'm burned by love
like a fire-frayed,
heat-chewed
rope-pipe.

Acknowledgements

I would like to thank the following people for their patient and selfless help in the finding and translating of the poems in this book.

Afghanistan: Assadullah Aimal Jadder, and staff of the Consulate of Afghanistan, Canberra.

Albania: Michael Portas, Rita Kelly.

Algeria: Heather and Saul Goode, Blanca Madani.

Andorra: Richard Hacken, Staff of the National Library of Andorra, Anna Platt, Eleanor Davidson, Alberto Jose Miyara. With permission.

Angola: Michael Cruz, Lisa Martin, Mary Jay.

Antigua & Barbuda: Lester Browne, Myrna Teirrel, Joseph Harden, M. Wyatt.

Argentina: Lisa Martin, Rebecca Allan.

Armenia: Dorli Meek.

Australia: Lorna MacIntosh, Misty Plummer, Alex Bishop.

Austria: Kurt Ganzl, Markus Jaigirder.

Azerbaijan: Azer H. Hasret, Betty Blair, Dr Mehmet Kara.

Bahamas: Kamau Braithwaite, Lester Browne, Myrna Teirrel, Eden Marshall.

Bahrain: Abdul Kalam Azad.

Bangladesh: Latifa Das, Harjit Gill, Peter Ramsey, Jafor Iqbal.

Barbados: Rovetta McKinney, Michael Estin.

Belarus: Rashed Chowdhury, Maria Tchooudkhouri.

Belgium: Gregory Beaven, Kurt Ganzl, Heather Goode.

Belize: Silvana Woods.

Benin: David Mahundiri, Brenda and Malcolm Ginever.

Bhutan: Tashi Delek, Professor Dr George van Driem, David Yang.

Bolivia: Eva Asensio Vicente, Lisa Martin.

Bosnia-Herzegovina: Ziva Pecavar, Merica Delic.

Botswana: B.J. Sefhako, Brenda and Malcolm Ginever, B.A. Gathousi, Botswana Department of Youth and Culture.

Brazil: Celia Martin, Audrey Cooper, Sue Lawley.

Brunei: Lee Bledisloe, Alex Burgin.

Bulgaria: Tamara Romanyk, Frederick Spencer.

Burkina Fasso: Saul Goode, Kurt Ganzl.

Burundi: Etienne Karekezi, Richard Blecker.

Cambodia: Carole Gibson, Anne Swann, Dr Zaniah Marshallsay.

Cameroon: Kurt Ganzl, Christophe Mirambeau, Kenneth Wilburn, Aliko Songolo.

Canada: Kurt Ganzl, Gregory Beaven, Tim Rauenbusch.

Cape Verde Islands: Krystyna Ziemba, Jose Barros, Gunga Tavares. With permission.
Central African Republic: Saul Goode, Alan Brierly, M.J. Bormann.
Chad: Alan Brierly, S. Wendo, Saul Goode.
Chile: Lisa Martin, Eva Asensio Vicente.
China: P.L. Win, Alek Stamnitz, Peter Aldman.
Colombia: Carole Gibson, Lisa Martin, Eleanor Davidson.
Comoros: Martin Ottenheimer, Carole Beckett, Eric Milan, Simon Young, Eva Mallenby, Kurt Ganzl, Christophe Mirambeau.
Congo (Brazzaville): Kurt Ganzl, Gregory Beaven.
Costa Rica: Anne Swann, Carole Gibson.
Croatia: Ursula Hobday, Ziva Pecavar, Merica Delic.
Cuba: Eva Asencio Vicente, C. Vale, Paul Estevin.
Cyprus: George Emba, Maria Henson, Elpida Kyriakide, Eleftherios Papaleontiou.
Czech Republic: Dorli Meek, Ziva Pecavar, Josef Pettersen.
Democratic Republic of the Congo: Gregory Beaven, Christophe Mirambeau.
Denmark: Maria Palmer, Asa Winter, Peter Hansen.
Djibouti: Saul Goode, Kurt Ganzl, Christophe Mirambeau, Ronald Squires, Harry B. Dunbar. With permission.
Dominica: Meagan Pfelz, J.P. Coyne, Lester Browne.
Dominican Republic: Eleanor Davidson.
East Timor: Malcolm Watkins, Dino Haddia, Phillip Waynes.
Ecuador: Lisa Martin, Jenny and Thomas Boarder, Lisandro Pena.
Egypt: from a dual hieroglyphic/English text by Rev H. Younde (1892).
El Salvador: Eleanor Davidson.
England: no help.
Equatorial Guinea: P. Nbe Ondo.
Eritrea: Ed Allison, M. Veya, Wilson Berra.
Estonia: Gris Klamas, Tina Ritson, National Library of Estonia.
Ethiopia: Alan Brierly.
Fiji: Samuel Kila, Martin Barwood.
Finland: Phoebe Ravenhall, Marja Heininen, Ursula Hobday.
France: Gregory Beaven, Kurt Ganzl.
French Guiana: Kurt Ganzl, Christophe Mirambeau.
Gabon: Alan Brierly, Dr F. Murphy.
Gambia: Alan Brierly; Leonard Allen, B.L. Surley.
Georgia: Tamara Romanyk, Dorli Meek.
Germany: Kurt Ganzl, Markus Jaigirder.
Ghana: R. Mossen.
Greece: Con Wilde, Maria Henson.
Grenada: Lester Browne, Myrna Teirrel.

Guatemala: Eleanor Davidson.

Guinea: Jim Yarris, Kurt Ganzl, Gregory Beaven, Saul Goode.

Guinea-Bissau: Mick Henson, Alois Berma.

Guyana: Martha Belton, Kurt Ganzl, Jim Yarris, F. Silai.

Haiti: Carrol F. Coates, Hannah Bourgein, Kurt Ganzl, Pierre Laleau. With permission.

Honduras: Carole Gibson, Anne Swann, Lee Weingast.

Hungary: Helen Bell, Nike Koos, Adam Horvath, Zsofia Zachar, Zsuzsanna Rozsafalvi, Vasy Geza.

Iceland: no help.

India: Sunil Sidpara, Esfandiar Kiani.

Indonesia: Tracey Yuan, Peter Lennon.

Iran: Dr K. Young, Roya Colandier.

Iraq: Malika, Yusuf and Latifa.

Ireland: Colin Thewley.

Israel: Sam Gordon, Alex Emmanar, Colin Foster.

Italy: Gregory Beaven, Favorita '68.

Ivory Coast: Charles Dendi, S. Marne.

Jamaica: Janet Williams, Lester Browne, Cleveland Thompson.

Japan: Phoebe Ravenhall, Hiroko Ohara, Mitsuko Ishino, Wakiko Tsujimoto.

Jordan: Lubna Khader, Mohammed Attiyah.

Kazakhstan: Nathan Lite, Charles Carlsson, Dana Ziyasheva.

Kenya: Alan Brierly, Malcolm and Brenda Ginever.

Kiribati: K. Thosi.

Korea (North): Kim Fulton, Ms Sunyoung Yi, Brother Anthony.

Korea (South): Kim Fulton, Ms Sunyoung Yi, Brother Anthony.

Kuwait: Abdul Kalam Azad.

Kyrgyzstan: Dr Tamer Yazircioglu, A. Valderin, Alec Sett.

Laos: Anne Swann, Caroline O'Sullivan.

Latvia: Tamara Romanyk, Sharon Strauch.

Lebanon: Michael Maguire, Nezahat Iplici.

Lesotho: Alan Brierly.

Liberia: Patricia Jabbeh Wesley, Andy Cox, Serone Bell.

Libya: Abdul Kalam Azad, Ibrahim Ighneiwa.

Liechtenstein: Ursula Hobday, Kurt Ganzl, Colin Brown, Barbara Vogt. With permission.

Lithuania: Tamara Romanyk, Dorli Meek, Terese Gustiene, Alfredas Zalys, Justinas Marcinkevicius. With permission.

Luxembourg: Kurt Ganzl, Christophe Mirambeau, Gregory Beaven, Pascal Nicolay, Germaine Goetzinger. With permission.

Macedonia: Broz Koneski.

Madagascar: Celia Martin, Audrey Cooper, W. Ender.

Malawi: Nick Downes, David Edgens, William Delaney.

Malaysia: Billy Saan, Tracey Yuan, P. Barsten.

Maldives: Majid Rasheed, Ed Roplin.

Mali: Alan Brierly, Saul Goode, M. Ellison.

Malta: Tamara Romanyk, Xenia Broughton, Dorli Meek, Emma Priest, Steven Ostermann.

Marshall Islands: Dirk Spennemann, Jane Downing.

Mauritania: Saul Goode, P. Ellis, Paul Boorde, Kurt Ganzl, Olivier Barlet.

Mauritius: Gregory Beaven, Kurt Ganzl.

Mexico: Lisa Martin, Lee Weingast, Lisandro Pena.

Micronesia: Edward Astley, Mo Alexander, Karun Badel.

Moldova: Chris Constantinescu, Phoebe Ravenhall.

Monaco: Anne Swann, Favorita '68.

Mongolia: Susie Drost, The Mongolian Society of Indiana, Bat-Erdene Batbayar, S. Erdenebat, Clare Eaton.

Morocco: El-Houssaine Baali, Colin and Ursula Hobday.

Mozambique: Sophia and Martin Balas.

Myanmar: S.L. Lee, Colin Wilberts, Wendy North.

Namibia: Alan Brierly.

Nauru: Ross Arthur, Steve Trussell, Solange Petit Skinner.

Nepal: Phoebe Ravenhall, Karuna Shashi, Sunita Khadgi, Binil Aryal, Pallav Ranjan. With permission.

Netherlands: Gary, Francina vanderLinden.

New Zealand: Lorna MacIntosh, Nancy Gallas, Kurt Ganzl, Ian Bevan, Tai Walker, Bill Matthews.

Nicaragua: Eleanor Davidson.

Niger: Jim Schneider, Peter Easton, Kathleen Hill, 'The Friends of Niger.'

Nigeria: Alan Brierly, B. Ouane.

Norway: no help.

Oman: Abdul Kalam Azad.

Pakistan: Nasreen Shaikh, Harjit Gill, V. Allison.

Palau: John Ellman, Ashley Barai.

Panama: Estelle Norden, Billy Galdes, P. Wynne.

Papua New Guinea: Edward Etepa, Nancy Gallas, Daniel Perissa, Kate Webster, Albert Wendt.

Paraguay: Eleanor Davidson.

Peru: Lisa Martin, Lisandro Pena, Dave French.

Philippines: Andrew Wegley, Lou Arthurs.

Poland: Katarzyna Pollonska, Sue Eley.

Portugal: Lester Browne, Audrey Cooper, Celia Martin, Becca, Patti Oliver.

Qatar: Abdul Kalam Azad, Dr Eric Howarth.

Romania: Chris Constantinescu, Phoebe Ravenhall, Dio Marescu, Helen Wilson.

Russia: Tamara Romanyk.

Rwanda: Alan Brierly.

Samoa: Albert Mahera, F.A. Allworth.

San Marino: Alessandro Della Balda, Robert Gasparoni.

São Tomé and Principe: Simon Lewis, Krystyna Ziemba.

Saudi Arabia: unknown, at the Markfield Islamic Institute.

Scotland: Helen Bell and mother, Patti Oliver.

Senegal: Gregory Beaven, Kurt Ganzl, Saul Goode, Lilyan Kesteloot, Jean-Marie Volet, Kenneth Wilburn, Aliko Songolo, Eileen Julien, Nene Ndiaye Diop.

Seychelles: Tim Hillier, Alan Starr, P. Alleyne, Christopher Morau, Jean-Claude Mahoune, Terence Madeleine.

Sierra Leone: Haike Frank, Abioseh Michael Porter.

Singapore: Anne Swann, Dr Zaniah Marshallsay, Kitty Yuen Ching.

Slovakia: Tamara Romanyk, Ziva Pecavar, Ursula Hobday.

Slovenia: Ziva Pecavar, Merica Delic, Ursula Hobday.

Solomon Islands: Amber Rawlins, Nancy Gallas, Janet Leake, Albert Wendt, Julian Maka'a.

Somalia: Ali Nazret, Una Awis, Michael Eastman.

South Africa: Joost Daalder, Alistair Turner, Peter Daskler.

Spain: Lisa Martin, Jenny and Thomas Boarder, Becca.

Sri Lanka: P. Gavanna.

St Kitts and Nevis: Lester Browne, Myrna Teirrel, Rob Holden.

St Lucia: Lester Browne, Edward Kandy, P. Ensor.

St Vincent and the Grenadines: Owen Forrest, Pila Cahanna.

Sudan: Alan Brierly.

Suriname: Rob Fikki, Ginger Thornton.

Swaziland: Alan Brierly, Rowena Astill, Abigail Herzen.

Sweden: Stephen Alexandersson, Trudi Hindle, Max Griffin.

Switzerland: Kurt Ganzl, Markus Jaigirder, Monique Tyler.

Syria: Ali Mahmud Taha.

Taiwan: Greg Gao, Lee Sombur.

Tajikistan: Esfandar Kiani, Darius Irandust, Hafiz Boboyorov, Dave Straub.

Tanzania: Malcolm and Brenda Ginever, Badisa Macasi, Kgosi Puleng.

Thailand: Tracey Yuan, Vince Akland.

Togo: G. Basuti, M. Seane, Evan Palle.

Tonga: Konai Thaman, Elizabeth Wood-Ellem, Okusi Mahina, Futa Helu, Helen Morton, Erica Mehrtens, Marcia Gilchrist, Daniel Longstaff.

Trinidad and Tobago: Cheryl Borde, Emma Gonzalez.

Tunisia: Saul Goode, Kurt Ganzl.

Turkey: Nevin Ipek, Dr Tamer Yazircioglu, Nazim and Fatih.

Turkmenistan: Nezahat Iplici, Emile Tremont.

Tuvalu: Milly Orpen, Mike and Allison Jordan.

Uganda: E.M. Dipuo.

Ukraine: Tamara, Dmytro and Iryna Romanyk.

United Arab Emirates: Mounther Alogaily, Cee Kassen.

Uruguay: Lisa Martin, Carole Gibson.

USA: Harmon Jenkin, Walter Andeis, Donald Luskett.

Uzbekistan: Hafiz Boboyorov, Tanju Cataltepe, Akram Tairovich Khabibullaev, Shawn Lyons. With permission.

Vanuatu: Nick Thieberger, Ralph Regenvanu, Albert Mahera.

Vatican City: Favorita '68, Massimo Ceresa, Pyotr Vincent. With permission

Venezuela: Eleanor Davidson.

Vietnam: Sally Yang, Mr and Mrs S. Goldenhall, Elisa Joy Holland, Duong Thu Huong.

Wales: Jenny Boarder, Evan Watson.

Yemen: F. Josephs, Silke Werner.

Yugoslavia: Ziva Pecavar, Merica Delic, Ursula Hobday, Sladjana Josic, Kurt Ganzl, Ljubica Marasanov.

Zambia: Daniel A. Reboussin, M. Sello, Mrs G. Ben.

Zimbabwe: Ursula Hobday, Jenny Ako, S. Lundberg, Micha Graham.

All the unnamed people who helped via the Internet.

Help finding people to find people: Patricia Murphy, Quinlin Mars, Edna Phillips, Peggy Wishart, Chris Jones.

Two years of encouragement: Gregory Beaven, Michael Schmidt, Sandra Grimes, Jenny Clark, Kurt Ganzl, Nancy Gallas.

Permission to use his notebook of African poems with his own translations (where acknowledged above): Alan Brierly.

Help from the following libraries: Coalville, Derby, Leicester, Birmingham, British Library, Nelson and Richmond (New Zealand).

The poems were turned first into a plain, literal, line-by-line English text by people acknowledged above, then re-poemed by me.

None of the poems was chosen by me. Each one was sent by a contributor or chosen by a translator from what they or I had found.

The countries of the world are as listed on pages 3, 4 and 5 of the *Collins World Atlas 2000*, with Scotland and Wales added.